The Runway of Life

The Runway of Life

by Peter Legge
with
Tashon Ziara

EAGLET PUBLISHING

Eaglet Publishing
Peter Legge Management Co. Ltd.
4th Floor, 4180 Lougheed Highway
Burnaby, British Columbia, V5C 6A7 Canada
Tel. (604) 299-7311 Fax (604) 299-9188

Library and Archives Canada Cataloguing in Publication

Legge, Peter, 1942-

The runway of life/by Peter Legge with Tashon Ziara
ISBN 0-9695447-5-8 (bound) — ISBN 0-9695447-4-X (pbk)
1. Self-actualization (Psychology) I. Ziara, Tashon II. Title
BF637.58L4536 2004 158.1 2004-904991-7

Jacket design by Catherine Mullaly; cover photo by
Bryan Reinhart/Masterfile; image manipulation by Debbie Craig
Typeset by Ina Bowerbank; Edited by Kim Mah
Printed and bound in Canada by Friesen Printers

Other books by the Author

How to Soar With the Eagles

You Can If You Believe You Can

It Begins With A Dream

If Only I'd Said That

Who Dares Wins

If Only I'd Said That: Vol. II

Booklets

97 Tips on How to Do Business in Tough Times

97 Tips on Customer Service

97 Tips on How to Jump-start Your Career

Acknowledgements

It was poet John Donne who penned the famous lines, "No man is an island, entire of itself." No one is successful unless others want them to be. No one, in my opinion, can write and publish a book without the support, encouragement and wisdom of many.

This book, my seventh, is a team effort by some extraordinarily talented individuals who have influenced me and worked with me to create the final volume you hold in your hands.

Firstly, thank you to my dear friend and mentor Joe Segal for the inspiration behind this book, and the permission to use his words in the title, *The Runway of Life*.

And warmest thanks to Joe's wife Rosalie, who has seen fit not only to encourage me in my endeavours in business and life, but who has also become a dear friend. No one could ask for a more loyal and faithful supporter.

I am also grateful to Darcy Rezac, managing director of The Vancouver Board of Trade, and Carole Taylor, president of CBC, who persuaded me to take the helm of The Vancouver Board of Trade as its chair from 2002 to 2003. The experience exposed me to a new and exciting business life that I could only have dreamt of.

It was during my tenure at The Board of Trade that I met Tashon Ziara, who carefully scripted my Board messages and speeches and brought life to my words and thoughts. Tashon ultimately became the skilled editor of *The Runway of Life,* and her contribution to a project of this scope was indispensable.

I would also like to thank all the folks at Canada Wide Magazines & Communications Ltd. who helped me to put this book together. Janice Maxwell has been my executive assistant for 17 years. She keeps my business and speaking life, as well as my charity work, as balanced as she can with her wonderful sense of humour.

Editor Kim Mah is a quiet but true professional and without a doubt the best in the business. Senior art director Cathy Mullaly, *BCBusiness* magazine's creative genius, designed the cover, while master scanning and imaging technician Debbie Craig added the final touches. Expert typesetter Ina Bowerbank brought her considerable skills to the task. And Corinne Smith, our vice president of production, performed an amazing feat in keeping us on time and on budget.

And thank you to the many, many leaders in our community who have given me freely of their time, and offered their advice whenever I needed it. No one can make it on his own. I didn't, and I am truly thankful to everyone who has helped me along the way.

Peter Legge
Vancouver, B.C.

Table of Contents

INTRODUCTION

Of Heroes and Giants — A Tale of Three Mentors

When my parents Bernie and Winnifred Legge emigrated from London, England, to Vancouver, Canada, about 50 years ago, it was a major turning point on their runway of life.

Disenchanted with postwar England, they set out on an amazing adventure to improve their lives and hopefully give their only son (me) a better opportunity on his runway of life.

Both of my parents have since passed away — my mother lived to be 77 years old and my father's runway ended at 85 years of age — however, in the time that we had together, they taught me well. They often told me, "If you want to be successful in life, Peter, associate yourself with successful people and model their behaviour. Observe their character traits and apply the very best to your own life. Be happy, have integrity, follow through, never lie, cheat or steal, stay married for life, love your children unconditionally, treat them like VIP guests in your home, because one day like all other guests, they too will leave. Serve the community with your own gifts and talent and maybe, just maybe, if you don't hit too many potholes along the way, you might be successful. Even if you are not successful at first, above all, never quit. Change direction if you must, but never quit!"

Pretty sound advice. So, with a solid marriage (36 years and counting) and three spectacular daughters, the stage was set to associate myself with successful people.

Now, if you have heard me speak before or read any of my other six books, you know I am very keen on mentors. This is primarily due to the fact that I have been blessed to have received much support and encouragement throughout my career.

In fact, I credit three men with having a great influence on my life. I call them my mentors. They give freely to me of their wisdom, experience and understanding of life. They also give to me the most precious thing they own — time on their runway of life and I am so very grateful to them all.

So who are they? My first mentor is Raymond J. Addington, O.B.E., former president of Kelly Douglas Co. Ltd., who is retired and living in Langley. Ray taught me the significance of character and follow-through.

My second mentor is Dr. Mel Cooper, C.M., O.B.C., LL.D. (Hon), owner of CFAX Radio in Victoria. I first met Mel when I worked at CKNW before I was married.

Mel taught me the importance of a good attitude. He once told me, "Your attitude determines your altitude. How high you want to go is almost entirely due to a positive attitude."

My third mentor is Dr. Joseph Segal, C.M., O.B.C. LL.D. (Hon), the legendary businessman and philanthropist who taught me the importance of communication, sharing ideas and never giving up.

Mentors are people who choose you as much as you choose them, and these three men have been in my corner for many years. Nobody is really successful unless other people want them to be. My mentors speak well of me, and my responsibility is to lead a life that models the lessons they have taught me and to reflect the qualities that they have bestowed on, and nurtured in me.

The need to associate with successful leaders is imperative on the runway of life. Lord Chesterfield said, "We are more than 50 per cent of who and what we are based on the role models that we pick. Therefore, it is important to be very careful which models we choose."

These three guys are faultless in their characters and in their reputations and with each of them, my relationship evolved over time into one where their advice and influence became invaluable in my life.

This book is dedicated to all three of my mentors, but it was inspired most of all by Joe Segal, who taught me the concept of the Runway of Life. Next to my father, Joe has been the most influential man in my life. He has never turned me down for a meeting, lunch, dinner or at any other time that I have sought his advice. He has modelled a life of integrity and above all, loyalty, devotion to family, and sound business practice. He has been a servant of the community (Vancouver) and the country (Canada) he calls home.

One of my first duties when I became Chairman of The Vancouver Board of Trade was to award Joe and his lovely wife Rosalie with the Community Leadership Award. I was also privileged to deliver the keynote address at the award luncheon. I would like to share with you part of the speech I gave that day. I believe it will give you some insight into the man that Joe is.

The philosopher Joseph Campbell once said, "It is not enough to say NO to things that frighten us. We must find worthwhile causes to which we care to say YES."

For many years, Joe and Rosalie Segal have cared enough that they have found literally dozens upon dozens of worthwhile causes that they have had the courage to say "Yes" to. Joe and Rosalie, you have modelled for all of us an amazing life.

George Washington Carver said, "When you can do the common things in life in an uncommon way, you will command the attention of the world."

Joe, when you thought no one was looking, we saw you serve your country in the Second World War. We felt your patriotism.

When you thought no one was looking, we saw you begin your career with no more than $800. We didn't know how determined you were.

When you thought no one was looking, we saw you marry the beautiful Rosalie Wosk and stay married for 50 years. We understood what commitment meant to you.

When you thought no one was looking, we saw your dedication to your four children, Sandra, Tracy, Lorne and Gary. We recognized how valuable the family is.

When you thought no one was looking, we saw you stop the car to let Rosalie place some money in a needy person's hand. We were impacted by your compassion.

When you thought no one was looking, we saw you help dozens of business people in this town as you dispensed your wisdom from your table at Chartwell restaurant. We were moved by your spirit.

When you thought no one was looking, we saw one fundraising dinner after another held in your home to benefit organizations like the Red Cross, St. John Ambulance, Vancouver Symphony Orchestra, The David Foster Foundation, Variety Club, Children's Help Line and the United Way. We realized how much you care.

When you thought no one was looking, we saw you calmly write a cheque to Simon Fraser University for $1 million. We understood what it meant to give until it hurts.

When you thought no one was looking, we saw you buy this very building [the historic Bank of Montreal building located at Granville and Pender in downtown Vancouver] and then turn around and give it to Simon Fraser University to establish a graduate school of business. We saw what citizenship looks like. It looks like Joe and Rosalie Segal.

And when you thought no one was looking, we watched in amazement and truly marvelled at your lifetime of giving and serving your community, your city and your country.

Stephen Grellet said, "I expect to pass through this world but once. Any good, therefore, that I can do, or any kindness that I can show to any fellow creature, let me do it now. Let me not defer or neglect it, for I shall not pass this way again."

I hope you enjoy this book; it is a celebration of the great spirit that Joe Segal embodies. He truly is a great friend and a great mentor.

CHAPTER 1

The Runway of Life — Joe's Story

I have known Joe Segal for almost 40 years and he has influenced my life as a role model and mentor for the past 20.

I first met Joe when I was in my early twenties selling radio advertising for CJOR. At that time, Joe had a little office in the back of one of his Fields department stores in downtown Vancouver. One thing I noticed back then was that the door to his office was always open. Joe didn't believe in putting barriers between himself and his employees. It's something that I made note of because it speaks to the character of the man.

So, every few weeks, I'd stop in at the store and Joe would invite me into his office where I'd make my pitch for him to buy an advertising spot. And in his straightforward manner, every time I showed up, Joe would tell me, "Kid, I admire your persistence, but I'm not going to buy anything from you."

Maybe a less thickheaded kid would have given up, not

me. I kept going back to visit Joe, even after I moved on from the radio station and eventually started my own company, Canada Wide Magazines & Communications Ltd.

Over the years I have turned to Joe for guidance and advice on matters of both a business and personal nature. And while I struggled with my first company, I watched Joe build an empire.

From humble beginnings with one store in 1950, he built a corporate chain of 70 Fields stores. In 1976, the year I started Canada Wide, that corporation acquired Zellers and eventually became a large shareholder of the Hudson's Bay Company.

As the years turned into decades, those visits became a habit that I think both Joe and I enjoyed. Often they would take place over lunch at Chartwell restaurant in the Four Seasons Hotel in downtown Vancouver where Joe is such a fixture that he has his own table.

During many of those lunches, when there wasn't a particular issue at hand, I enjoyed sitting back and listening to Joe talk about his life and the lessons that experience has taught him. It was over one of these lunches, while Joe was expanding on his philosophy of life, that I got the idea for this book.

"Many people think of life as a road or a highway," Joe told me that day. "And that may be true in so much as there are many unexpected twists and turns and sometimes you get lost or end up at a destination that wasn't on the map. But if you think about it, a highway can go on forever, and life isn't like that. Life is more like a runway — because at some point you're going to run out of asphalt."

At this point, Joe picked up a napkin off the table and drew a horizontal line across it. At the beginning of the line he put a zero and at the end of the line he put the number 90. "That's how old I expect to be when I meet my maker," he said. Next, Joe wrote his current age on the line and turned to me. "The part of the line between zero and your current age, that's history, it's done, so forget about it."

Then he pointed to the section of the line between his current age and where he expects his runway to end. "The distance between where I am now and the end of my runway, that's all I've got to work with. So I have to ask myself, 'What am I going to do with the time that I have?' and whatever my answer is to that question, that's what I need to stay focused on."

I looked down at the napkin in Joe's hand and saw how short that section of the line was, then I thought about my own runway and started to break it down. If I'm fortunate enough to live to 90 years, that means just 25 more birthdays, 25 Christmas dinners with my family and 25 more glorious summers.

I realized in that moment that Joe was right, no matter what we have accomplished in the past — or how successful we have been — what really matters is the time we have ahead of us and what we choose to do with what is left of our runway of life. In that one simple yet powerful illustration, Joe had summed it up, and I told him right then, "This is a compelling idea and it would make a great book."

It has also become one of the key messages in my speaking engagements where I start out by drawing the runway on a piece of paper or a white board and filling in some numbers. Then, reminding my audience that all of our runways come to an end — sometimes with little or no warning — I ask them, "How much time are you willing to waste?"

While it can be frightening to consider how little time you have left on your own runway of life, it can also be motivating. We need to remember that although we can't slow down time, we can take control of how we use it. And that's why I've written this book.

The Runway of Life was inspired by Joe Segal. Joe is an original. Perhaps that is due in part to losing his father at a young age, or maybe it was something in the water in that small town of Vegreville, Alberta, where he grew up. Whatever the reason, early in life Joe made the decision to use only what works for him, to build an extraordinary life and to set an example that others could follow.

I've heard it said that great companies are not built by individuals who rely on somebody else to take care of them. They are built by men and women who rely on themselves, who dare to shape their own lives, who have enough courage to blaze new trails. Individuals with enough confidence in themselves to take the necessary risks. When Joe left Vegreville as a young man to come to Vancouver, friends said, "It's so big you can't succeed." Joe said, "It's so big I can't miss."

The world is in need of leaders. Countries need leaders. Businesses need leaders. Communities need leaders and families need leaders.

Joe has often said to me that one of life's problems is not that we aim too high and fail. It is that we aim too low and succeed. No one could ever accuse Joe of aiming too low; he is an inspiration to me and everyone else who has had the good fortune to benefit from his generosity of spirit and his wisdom.

In every field of endeavour, be it the building of his business empire, his contributions to the United Way and so many other good causes, his championship of Simon Fraser University or his wise counsel, Joe's stamp of leadership is everywhere.

"If I can do it, anyone can do it," he often tells me.

That's leadership, that's Joe.

Hopefully, as you read through these pages, the stories and ideas presented within will resonate with you and help to illuminate your own unique path along the runway of life. Along with the wealth of other thoughts and insights I've collected in this book, I invite you to explore Joe's philosophy with me and wish you a safe journey.

CHAPTER 2

How Time Flies on the Runway of Life

The great Greek physician Hippocrates (460-357 BC) once said, "The life so short, the craft so long to learn."

How right he was and still is. Life is indeed very short.

In the Hollywood movie *Cleopatra,* with stars Rex Harrison as Caesar, Elizabeth Taylor as Cleopatra and Richard Burton as Mark Antony, there is a memorable scene about halfway through it where Antony says to his arch rival, "When you die, Octavian, you will die without ever having been alive."

I read sometime ago in *USA Today* that if we are really lucky, doctors can keep us alive until we are 85 years old. Obviously, a healthy diet, reasonable amount of exercise, good attitude and active lifestyle increase our chances of living until 85 years of age. In addition, a more recent report in the same publication claimed that if we keep a positive attitude and live to 60, we will have suffered no chronic illness. This shows that there is definitely a health benefit to a positive attitude in life.

Now, living to 85 years may sound like a pretty long time for anyone under the age of 40, but in fact, it is only 4,420 weeks. Doesn't sound so long now, eh? (as we Canadians would say).

Although we all start at the same point — we are all born — we don't all have the same amount of time to work with. So how long is your Runway of Life? When do you think it will end?

0____X

The Runway of Life

If you think your life will end at 85 years and you are now 55, then you have 30 years left on your Runway of Life. Take a moment to do the math for your own life.

Perhaps you are married with three children and approaching Freedom 55. You are successful, have matured your RRSPs, have sufficient savings and investments and are ready for the good life! So what does that look like for you?

What's left is vitally important and what you do and how you handle those years, months, weeks, days and hours is equally important. You don't want to look back and say, "If only I'd done this." You want to look back and say, "I'm glad I did this. I risked and I won!"

If I were to ask any one of you reading this book, "Do you want to waste your life?" I would be surprised if anyone said, "Yes."

How about a decade? Nope.

How about a year? Nope again.

How about a month or a week? Still no.

But how about a day?

Well, a day, big deal! Most people don't value a single day all on its own. They think they have so many to waste that "it's no big deal."

Well, a day quickly becomes a week. A week becomes a month, then a year. Before we know it a decade has passed and soon we realize that we have more life behind us than before us — and we still haven't learned the value of a day and its importance to our entire life.

The truth is most of us waste at least a little bit of time every day without even thinking about it. We waste it by procrastinating, we waste it by doing work we aren't really passionate about, we waste it fighting with loved ones over things that aren't really important or wrestling with our conscience rather than taking care of the things that really are important.

So, how much time are YOU willing to waste: an hour, a day, a week, a year? As we can clearly see by the numbers on our own runway, it all adds up and the further we get along the runway, the faster we seem to be going.

To make matters even more pressing, consider the fact that we are all born to die and none of us knows for sure how long we've actually got on this Runway of Life. We don't have to look any further than the events of September 11, 2001, to know that it is true. And yet, it is a simple truth that most of us put out of our minds, one that is both a blessing and a curse.

I believe we must use this knowledge to motivate ourselves rather than allow fear to immobilize us or staunch our courage. It is a question of perspective, and the choice is ours. Ask yourself, "If tomorrow I am no longer here, what will I wish I had done differently this day, while I still had the chance?"

My wife Kay and I were in New York a few days before the second anniversary of what is now known around the world as 9/11. It was a glorious and brilliantly sunny Friday morning. Above us a lone commercial aircraft could be seen in the sky, en route to either Kennedy, Newark or LaGuardia airport. It was an eerie sight to say the least.

As we looked upon Ground Zero, a fenced-in area where the World Trade Center's twin towers had once stood, I couldn't help but think of where I was on that fateful day, and how it made me feel about the world I lived in.

Those who committed the ungodly acts of 9/11 wanted to disrupt the western world and our way of life. So even though I was so thankful to live in Canada and particularly Vancouver, I also realized that because New York is considered to be the centre of the world — particularly the financial centre of the free world — this tragedy was really devastating for all of us. The personal tragedy that resulted will be felt for many, many years to come, as thousands of families and friends continue to grieve for their loved ones.

On the day we were at the World Trade Center site, a New York CBS reporter was taping that day's noon news there and we struck up a conversation. She told me her husband had worked in one of the towers but was late for work on the day of the attacks. She shed a tear as she jumped into her van but turned to me and said, "I'll have to be gentle with him this week." As I turned to say goodbye I noticed a big sign hanging from a nearby building. It read:

The human spirit is not measured by the size of the act, but by the size of the heart

It is from the heart that wickedness springs, but so too does love and goodness. Let us never forget 9/11, and let us always remember the courage and the size of America's heart as the country wrestled with the forces of evil that could very well threaten all of us — even here in Vancouver. God Bless America!

Now, I want you to ask yourself again, "If tomorrow I am no longer here, what will I wish I had done differently this day, while I still had the chance?"

I was reading some comments written by a young entrepreneur in Toronto not long ago. He was talking about how our success in life is determined more by what we choose to focus our energy on each day than it is by being the first, the best or the brightest. He offered Terry Fox as an example, saying, "A one-legged kid with cancer runs halfway across Canada while millions complain that there's nothing on TV tonight."

Terry Fox died more than 23 years ago at the age of 22.

His runway wasn't very long. He was an average young man from an average Canadian family who decided to do something with the time that he had. Today, people all over the world know his name and run each year in honour of his Marathon of Hope to raise money for cancer research.

In our individual lives, we should feel great empowerment in the knowledge that our choices determine what is to be or not. And yet we would rather that someone else initiate, take the risk, do the groundwork and pave the way for us to follow at a comfortable distance. If Terry had waited, we would not know his name and millions of people with cancer would not have benefited from the research that his Marathon of Hope continues to fund. He is a great reminder that we must live our lives from the inside out.

I want to tell you another story on this same theme. It is about a rabbi who set out to change the world. After a time, he found that he wasn't making much progress, so he tried to change his country. This was also too difficult, so he tried to change his neighbourhood. When he didn't have success there, he tried to change his family. Even that was easier said than done, so he tried to change himself.

Then an interesting thing happened. When he had changed himself, his family changed. And when his family changed, his neighbourhood changed. When his neighbourhood changed, his country changed. And when his country changed, the world changed.

If you remember this story, whenever you are unhappy

with the state of your life, you will always know where to start to make it better. Mahatma Gandhi once said, "Be the change you want to see in the world."

Of course, sometimes it is easier to believe that we are powerless in a situation where we don't want to take responsibility for making a decision. Perhaps it is because secretly, we like the idea of a force we cannot resist or a situation we cannot prevent from developing.

Maybe this gives us an excuse to let events happen that we wouldn't publicly express a desire for — after all, someone's feelings might be hurt, it could go against tradition or just be plain unpopular.

When you think about it, it may be easier to cast yourself as a victim of circumstance than to declare yourself an architect of transformation. But which one do you want to be remembered as?

What will it take to shift us from the passive to the active? Will it take a disaster like 9/11, diagnosis of a life-threatening illness or the loss of an important relationship?

On this day you are not fully cut off from someone you love, but you could be tomorrow unless you take action today. Perhaps this day you still have body and soul together, but tomorrow you will not because of poor eating habits or a stress-filled lifestyle. Perhaps this day you have the opportunity to praise someone's accomplishment or thank someone for their hard work or speak the truth where it is needed; but tomorrow — for whatever reason — it will be too late.

Today . . . tomorrow. What a difference a day makes!

There is a saying that goes, "Live every day as if it were your last, because one day it will be." It is up to each of us to decide what to do with the time that we have.

Consider the difference a day could make if you set aside your fears and spent it learning to do something you dreamed about as a child (like singing in front of an audience or flying a plane). Imagine the difference a day could make if you turned off the television and spent it recording the stories of your elderly relatives or teaching a child to ride a bike.

It is our accomplishments and our shared experiences that add colour and texture to life.

I suspect that many of us go through life thinking and believing that we will live a long and productive life, so we continually put off making important changes — until the kids are older, or we've paid off the mortgage, or until retirement or . . . .

It doesn't make much difference what our end number is. If we are realistic and honest with ourselves, we know we will die at some point. This book *The Runway of Life* is not intended to discourage you. Rather, it is my hope to encourage you to do the most with what you have and to understand that we are not limited by what we can do, only by how much time we have to do it.

As Olympic psychologist Dr. Denis Waitley once said, "We are all born with the seeds of greatness." Therefore, all those seeds need to be planted and nurtured so that we become the very best we can be during our own Runway of Life.

We must maximize every day to do and be all we can, to contribute to life in its fullest. Many of us believe that there is a life after this and that Heaven awaits those who believe. I am one of those people.

However, it is our responsibility on earth to thoroughly exhaust the incredible opportunities that abound for all of us. Those opportunities stare us in the face every day. At the same time that windows of opportunity close, doors will open. We need to be ready to walk through them and experience all that life has to offer.

Nido Qubein, author and professional speaker, once told me that to be successful you need to walk hand in hand with those men and women who are more successful than you.

Nineteenth-century philosopher Arthur Schopenhauer observed, "Great minds are related to the brief span of time during which they live, as great buildings are to a little square in which they stand: you cannot see them in all their magnitude because you are standing too close to them."

And Alvin Toffler said, "You've got to think about big things while you're doing small things, so that all the small things go in the right direction."

I want to leave you with this one last story. Although I don't know who the author was, I think it bears repeating.

Once upon a time there was a wise man who used to go to the ocean to do his writing. He had a habit of walking on the beach before he began his work. One day he was walking along the shore. As he looked down the beach, he saw a human figure moving like a dancer. He smiled to himself to think of someone who would dance to the day.

So he began to walk faster to catch up. As he got closer, he saw that it was a young man and the young man wasn't dancing, but instead was reaching down to the shore, picking up something and very gently throwing it into the ocean.

As he got closer he called out, "Good morning! What are you doing?"

The young man paused, looked up and replied, "Throwing starfish in the ocean."

"I guess I should have asked, why are you throwing starfish in the ocean?" said the old man.

"The sun is up, and the tide is going out. And if I don't throw them in, they'll die," the young man responded.

"But, young man, don't you realize that there are miles and miles of beach, and starfish all along it. You can't possibly make a difference!"

The young man listened politely. Then bent down, picked another starfish and threw it into the sea, past the breaking waves and said, "It made a difference for that one."

There is something very special in each and every one of us. We have all been gifted with the ability to make a difference. And if we can become aware of that gift, we gain through the strength of our visions the power to shape the future.

We must each find our starfish. And if we throw our stars wisely and well, the world will be blessed.

CHAPTER 3

Joe's Pearls of Wisdom

If you haven't experienced the bottom, you wouldn't appreciate the top

Ever wonder why some of the most successful people in business — the ones who manage to stay on top for decades — are those who have, at one time or another, failed magnificently. I believe it is because experience is the best teacher and if you are really going to succeed at anything, you have to know how — when your big plan blows up in your face — to pick yourself up and start building again.

Never question who takes more, just give more

If you choose to focus on giving rather than taking — creating a sense that you have more than you need — you will always have an atmosphere of abundance in your life.

If you have love, it's easier

All in all, love is a rare commodity in this world. It doesn't come often. When it does we should be prepared to recognize it. If you are fortunate enough to find someone to love, consider what a privilege it is that this person has found you worthy of sharing their universe.

You must have a thirst for knowledge

The world is constantly changing. You must learn and grow continually to keep up. The most successful people avail themselves of every opportunity to learn. It matters not whether you were born rich or poor, knowledge is the great equalizer. No matter what you come from, if you pursue knowledge, it can change your fate.

Alone, you are only as good as your reach; you must join hands with others

Remember how as a child, whenever you went out, your parents told you to stick together and hold hands to cross the street. Well, nothing has changed. Joining up with others — sharing both risks and resources — gives us courage and allows us to play to our strengths, accomplishing far more than we would ever have imagined doing alone.

In most cases, a business fails because the guy at the top can't see the bottom

Hierarchies work great in the military, not so great in business. Having too many levels of management often means the person at the top — the one making the decisions — has no idea what the people in the trenches are thinking or doing. If you're in charge, make a point to keep communication flowing in both directions and get the word out that you have an open door policy.

Most people haven't planned for life after 65

You may think of age 65 and retirement as the ultimate goal in your life, but when it has come and gone, then what? Believe me, some of the best years of life come after 65, and yet, so many people do not plan for what they hope to accomplish during this time.

People complicate their own lives

Far too many people complicate their lives by worrying about little things and never really having any direction or purpose in what they do. My philosophy is very straightforward: the simplest way is the best way. Stick to the basics, stay focused on your goals, treat others with respect, speak the truth, be thankful for what you have and don't be afraid to help out others when you can. Keep in mind, as **simple** as it is, it will not always be **easy** — that's life for you!

I have low tolerance for people who are competent but don't show confidence

If you think you have no right to be successful, you are right! Lack of confidence is often a form of shame; it can be very debilitating to one's progress in life. Confidence is an acknowledgement of your self-worth. If you do not value yourself, others will follow your example and they will not value you either.

Why buy a high-powered car if you aren't going to drive it

I've always wondered about why someone would go out and buy a Jaguar or a Ferrari and then never use it to its potential. They drive around town at 30 kilometres per hour, afraid of a scratch or a ding. To me, that's making waste of a good car. What's the point? Life is meant to be lived and cars were made to be driven.

Everything is relative, some things are relevant and some things are not

It's not always easy to keep priorities in perspective; however, the ability to do so will be a great factor in determining how quickly you achieve your goals. Just as we must choose one specific career from the many, we must also be discerning about which situations we need to deal with personally, which we should delegate to others and which we should ignore altogether. Being able to filter out that which is not relevant frees us up to give more attention to what is important.

I'd rather have someone with experience and no money than someone with money and no experience

Money can be acquired without effort, experience cannot. Money comes and goes, but experience, once you gain it, is with you forever. Now, that's something you can take to the bank.

Always play to your advantage, know your strengths — and your weaknesses

Great leaders are those who, when faced with a challenge, can look within themselves, assessing both their strengths and their weaknesses and then take action or make strategic changes in accordance with what they see.

If I was starting out again today, I would look for an opportunity that is going to teach me something

In today's knowledge economy, most of your value is inside your head. That means whatever you learn in one job, you take it with you when you move on. If I was just starting out today, I would take advantage of this fact by looking for positions that would develop my technical skills. Opportunities often arise when you least expect them. My advice is to work hard and acquire as much knowledge and experience as you can, so when opportunity knocks, you will be ready for it.

Success is much more a matter of courage than of ability

Competing in business in today's increasingly globalized world is a battle of wits; more than ability, it requires courage. Courage is not the lack of fear, it is fear plus action. Courage comes from deep within the heart and flushes away the paralysis created by fear; it is the willingness to reach beyond one's comfort zone. Courage comes in many forms, not only from thoughts and deeds of greatness, but in the everyday art of being true to your word. It is a skill that can be learned and strengthened through practice and it begins with the question, "What would I be doing if I were 10 times bolder?"

Ultimately, it is persistence that will pay off, forget about perfection

For the most part, there simply isn't enough time on the runway of life for any of us to worry about perfection. Besides, perfection isn't about doing a good job; it is about being in control and an overbearing need to be right. It is a far better thing to be persistent; find a goal that captures your imagination and strive to achieve it.

Most of us will not choose how we will die, but we all choose — every day — how we will live

Free will is a beautiful thing, yet with it comes responsibility and accountability. The sum of your life rests on your shoulders. Only you can decide your fate through the priorities you set, the decisions you make, the efforts you spend, the sacrifices you make. What you choose for today will determine all of your tomorrows. Act accordingly!

Don't let your insights live with you rent-free — put them to work

When you have a good idea, act on it. An ounce of DOING is worth 10 pounds of PLANNING. It is my belief that most people will learn more and get closer to their goals by taking action and learning what works and what doesn't work for them.

Expect to win

If you believe that you will win, you are already halfway there. The most common thing that holds us back is our own negative thoughts or expectations.

One of life's problems is not that we aim too high and fail; it is that we aim too low and succeed

Just as trying to accomplish too much can lead to exhaustion and burnout, setting your goals too low can lead to complacency, meandering and loss of interest. If we do not have to reach and go beyond what we believe we are capable of, there is no sense of accomplishment and no growth as a result of our success. No one rises to low expectations.

The common traits among all successful people are desire, determination and confidence

Desire provides the motivation to get you started, determination keeps you going when you encounter obstacles, and confidence gives you the courage to see it through to the end, even when others don't believe in you.

Too many times in life we see a need, but hesitate to act on it

Believe it or not, the best opportunities don't come in a package with a bow. In fact, more often they present themselves in the form of a problem. Successful people are those who are willing to put their neck on the line and take a risk — they see a need and act decisively to find a way to fulfill it.

In all things, be bold

Leaders with a bold approach usually build far higher morale than those with a defensive outlook. They actively encourage their people to use their initiative and "give it a go." They expect and accept failures, but don't reward those who do nothing and never risk failing.

Do not brood or bottle things up, problems don't disappear, they have to be worked on and worked out

When times get rough, many people make the mistake of withdrawing completely, trying to hide the problem from the rest of the world. This could make you very depressed and complicate or worsen your situation. The sooner you come to terms with your problem, the sooner you will be able to get back on top.

You aren't ready for the answer until you are ready to ask the question

Expecting someone else to solve your problems is unrealistic and you don't learn a damn thing from it. When you figure out what the question is, then you will be ready to find the answer.

CHAPTER 4

Why Do We Need Goals?

Here you are, setting off on your very first cross-country trip. You've packed up the car and you're ready to go. From the Golden Gate Bridge in San Francisco to New York — the city that never sleeps — and everything in between, you're going to see it all.

You back the car out of the driveway and you're off. You've already planned your first stop, the giant redwood forests of Oregon.

Not far into your trip, you realize you need to check the map because it seems you've missed the on-ramp to the freeway. You check the glove box and for a moment you panic because you realize you've forgotten your map.

After considering the problem for a few moments, you say the heck with it. You don't need a map, you know where you're going and you can always stop and ask others for directions along the way. You take a right, turn on the radio for company and keep on going. Unfortunately, you never reach your destination. You were heading the wrong way, but you were making good time.

Too many of us take this same approach to goal setting; we dream about where we want to go, but we don't have a map to get there.

What is a map? Essentially, it is the written word. What is the difference between a dream and a goal? That's right, the written word.

Of course, just as with a map, we need to do more than simply jot down some ideas on a piece of paper. Without putting some real thought and energy into formulating each goal, we are simply making a wish. Our goals need to be clear, complete and focused.

South Australia's highest-paid public speaker, Peter Daniels, president and founder of The World Centre for Entrepreneurial Studies, said in his best-selling book *How To Reach Your Life Goals*, that life must be measured in something more meaningful than time.

Goals give life its flavour. Goals give your life direction and purpose. You can't hit a target if you don't have one, and as the days turn into weeks and weeks into months, you begin to realize just how very important each and every day on this Runway of Life is in shaping your future.

My good friend and North America's top business speaker, Brian Tracy, says, "It's all about goals — everything else is commentary!"

An Ernst & Young study of 2003 said that the primary

focus of entrepreneurs is outward on expansion, rather than inward on structure and rules. How can we possibly look outward or, in fact, to the future unless we set goals in all aspects of our lives?

Entrepreneurs display an extraordinary, overwhelming determination to grow their business ventures. It is fundamental to their continuance and long-term success that entrepreneurs refuse to be distracted by roadblocks along the way. Goals have the ability to turn roadblocks into challenges to be solved or mountains to be climbed, conquered and left in the distance. They turn everything else, all of the noise and confusion, into background music that can be turned down or tuned out.

Therefore, measurable goals in business, health, wealth, spirituality and family are critical to our success.

Motivational speaker Zig Ziglar says we need to be meaningful specifics when most of us are meaningless generalities.

Peter Daniels also noted in his book that he has noticed that those who retire and have no further goals die or are confined to total medical care within a few short years. He also went on to say that those who retire in a positive way seem to slip into another gear, align their magnetic force to another pole and get a new lease on life. They extend their lives even further.

I like to ask my audiences, "How old would you be if you didn't know how old you were?"

My own father worked until the then-mandatory retirement age at his company — 65. I asked him to join me as I was beginning my own company, Canada Wide Magazines & Communications Ltd. Talk about a new lease on life! He worked for another 20 very positive years until his untimely death at 85. And while many his age were tired and worn out, he excelled at this new challenge and opportunity.

Goals can also be described as dreams, a vision, purpose, mission or passion. Earl Nightingale says that, "Success is the progressive realization of a worthy ideal." Those ideals are your goals.

Bob Richard once said that if you write on a 3 x 5 card what you intend to be in life — making it specific — and keep that card for constant reference and embed that goal deeply in your mind for a period of two years, you will become what you said you would. That which we constantly imagine will emerge as fact.

Thomas Edison can vitalize our intended goals with this quote, "If we did all the things we are capable of doing, we would literally astonish ourselves."

Only the top three per cent of business leaders write down their goals. So, if the universal law of "sowing and reaping" is to be believed and the universal principle, which is sometimes called the granddaddy of all universal laws, "We become what we think about most of the time," then writing down our "Top 10" goals and rereading them every day fits nicely into that particular law.

And guess what? If our goals are what we are thinking about every day, then it stands to reason that in the fullness of time we should reach our objective.

James Allan once said, "You will become as small as your controlling desire or as great as your dominant aspirations."

For many people, the goal is to become a millionaire. In fact, in your lifetime you should strive to become financially independent. If you saved $100 per month from the age of 20 to 65 and invested the money in a fund earning an average of 10 per cent per annum, you would be worth more than $1,000,000 by the time you retired. Almost anyone who really wanted to could save $100 per month.

Business guru Peter Drucker said, "We overestimate what we can accomplish in one year but underestimate what we can accomplish in five years."

So, looking to the future is important in your personal strategic planning. Begin today!

Here are some additional thoughts on having goals and five steps to get you started:

Goals are important, but most people don't have any. Proverbs 29:18 says, "Where there is no vision, the people perish."

1. Brainstorm.

Before you choose a single goal to set and focus on, use a blank sheet of paper to write down as quickly as possible all the things you want in a number of categories, such as:

family, career, educational, financial, physical, spiritual, social, etc. Once you have created a list, prioritize each of the items on your list. This will allow you to begin immediately focusing on the potential goals that are most important to you.

All leaders have vision. Vision is what motivates us to take present action. It also determines what we set as our goals in the short term (6 – 12 months), the midterm (3 – 5 years) and indeed, for our lifetime.

2. Make sure the goals you set are truly your own.

The purpose of setting goals is to focus and plan for what you want in your life, not to impress others.

Most people don't really know what they want and so they spend countless hours talking about what they don't want rather than what they do want.

3. Set only positive goals for yourself.

Because you want to be growing towards something, write down each of your goals in a positive statement rather than a negative one. Consider: "I will save to buy a home" is a positive goal, while "I will not spend money" is a negative goal. By focusing on the positive, you'll quit spending money because you'll be so focused on your goal that you won't notice you've stopped spending money. Using positive language attracts positive situations and people into your life.

Many people say that they are not passionate about life. Goals and purpose will give you passion and a reason to get up and on with the day.

4. Set a deadline for achieving each of your goals.

A goal is not a goal until you set a date for it. We have too many things to do in our lives; that's why so often only those with deadlines get accomplished. It is also important to have both long and short-term goals.

Oil billionaire H.L. Hunt said, "Success requires two things. You must know what you want and you must determine the price you are willing to pay to get it."

5. Don't try to go it alone — gather assistance.

It is important to identify the knowledge you will need to acquire and the people or organizations that could give you essential help as you work towards your goals.

CHAPTER 5

When Was the Last Time You Did Something for the First Time?

Much of the content of my presentations is based on stories from the experiences of my life and they usually end with a teaching point for my audiences. Based on this, the "Peter Legge Storytelling Award" was established and is awarded annually to a Canadian Association of Professional Speakers (CAPS) presenter who demonstrates eloquence in storytelling from the platform.

The first winner of this award, presented in 2003, was Linda Edgecombe, a wonderful author, speaker and humorist from Kelowna, British Columbia. If you've ever heard Linda, you know that this award was well deserved.

In recent years, I have had the privilege to share the platform with Linda a few times and I love her energy and enthusiasm, both of which are powerful elements in her communication with the audience.

In every speech I've heard Linda give, she asks the audience this insightful question: "When was the last time you did something for the first time?"

I have to tell you, this question really made me stop and take stock of all the firsts in my life: my first business, the first time I held each of my baby daughters in my arms, my first time on stage, the first time I was arrested, my first Jaguar automobile, the first time I spoke before the House of Commons, or the first time I flew from London to New York in less than four hours at 55,000 feet and twice the speed of sound on the British Airways Concorde. Now there was a first time that will never come again (the Concorde jets have since been retired) and I am thankful to have seized the opportunity.

Brian Trubshaw, Concorde's first pilot, said, "It is not unreasonable to look upon Concorde as a miracle." As we all know, miracles don't happen every day, but when they do, we need to be brave enough to stand up and seize hold of them. There is great power in firsts, it is the stuff of legends. You'll notice that people don't generally tell stories about the second time they went bungy jumping.

That is why, as we go through this short life, we must take advantage of the unique opportunities that come our way. For many of them will be once-in-a-lifetime chances as we travel along this runway of life. Opportunities which, when grasped, may just produce the equivalent of the "Butterfly Effect" in our lives.

For those of you who are not familiar with the Butterfly

Effect, it is an aspect of chaos theory in physics that refers to the discovery that in a chaotic system such as the global weather, tiny disturbances in one part of the system can sometimes lead to major changes in the larger system.

As the story goes, it is theoretically possible that a butterfly flapping its wings in Brazil could create tiny changes in the air flow that would lead to a tornado in Texas.

Of course, in most cases the flapping of a single butterfly's wings will make no difference whatsoever. But on the rare occasion when the system is at a point where it could go either way (like a spinning basketball balanced on the tip of your finger), the flapping may be just the difference that causes the future to unfold in another way.

That same principle applies to people. A decision made in one person's life can, on occasion, lead to major changes in society as a whole.

Take, for example, the story of Bill Gates and Microsoft. Throughout the 1970s and into the beginning of the 1980s, International Business Machines (IBM) remained firm in their resolve not to get involved in the personal computer market. According to executives in the company, the potential market was too small and not worth the effort.

However, with the success and rapid growth of companies like Apple, Atari and Commodore, they changed their mind.

There was just one problem. Before they could manufacture their own PCs, they needed a new disk operating system

(DOS). The existing IBM system was strictly for large mainframe computers. Rather than develop it themselves, IBM decided to hire a small company with experience in this area to write the software for them.

As owner of the small company, Mr. Bill Gates met with the IBM executive in charge to make a deal. And this is where the butterfly effect comes in, for rather than sell the system outright, Gates told IBM that he wanted a royalty on every DOS they sold.

After some contemplation, the executive decided that this was a fair deal given that IBM still believed that PCs would never be a really big market anyway. This decision alone most likely would have ensured Mr. Gates' future success, but the story doesn't end there.

Perhaps the beat of the butterfly's wing that changed the currents of history is the fact that the licensing agreement Mr. Gates made with IBM was a non-exclusive one.

In August 1981, IBM introduced their new line of microcomputers sporting Microsoft's DOS to almost immediate success.

Of course, this got the attention of other companies who, after some investigation, realized that they could clone the PC. So clone they did. And who do you suppose these companies turned to for an operating system to run their clones?

The rest, as they say, is history. Bill Gates became the richest man on the planet and Microsoft grew to dominate the software industry worldwide.

I believe we must take advantage of all the possibilities that life has to offer. All along the runway that is our life, each of us will be presented with opportunities that could change our course or perhaps even the course of history. We must seize these opportunities.

The great U.S. statesman Benjamin Franklin once said, "We have a long time to sleep when we're dead."

If not now, then when? The runway of life is getting shorter by the day. So ask yourself the question, "When was the last time I did something for the first time?"

CHAPTER 6

A Purposeful Life

How often have we said to ourselves in good times and in bad,

"Lord, why me?"

"Lord, why me?"

I believe there are two aspects of our lives that we can change to help address the feeling of helplessness that results in the above question. First of all, if you want good answers — specifically ones that you can work with to make your life more fulfilled and meaningful — then you have to ask good questions. As far as questions go, "Why me?" isn't a very useful one. Chances are, even if God did answer the question, that wouldn't be enough to satisfy you. You would still argue with God, and yourself, and miss the whole point altogether. "What is the point?" you ask. The point is, you already have all of the answers; you just have to ask **yourself** the questions. If you are unhappy, bored, tired or depressed, better to do a little soul searching of your own and ask yourself a few questions. Like, "When was the last time I felt happy or excited and what was the reason for it?" or "What have I been told I am really good at and how can I make that a bigger part of my life?" or even, "What is one thing I have always dreamed of doing but have been too afraid to try?"

Once we have some answers, we need to start applying them to our life. God may have given us our talents, but it is up to us to find a purposeful use for those talents. That is the gift of free will. You can only make a difference in this life and to your own life if you accept the challenge of finding and living for your own purpose.

One person's purpose, like Vancouver mogul Jimmy Pattison, might be to build a worldwide $5.5-billion empire employing 26,000 people. Another person's purpose, like my youngest daughter Amanda, might be to teach grade two students and to bring a smile to someone's face.

Either way, it is what we do to find our purpose and it is what we do with whatever talents and abilities we have been given. And then, if we are living for our purpose, we can inspire hope and fulfillment in others.

People who love what they do are more apt to be successful. When your purpose and your talent intersect with one another, the sky is the limit for your achievement in this life.

Last Father's Day my three daughters gave me a gift of a book — no socks or tie to be returned to the store, but a thoughtfully purchased book — Hillary Rodham Clinton's book *Living History*.

It is an account of her eight years as First Lady of the United States, living under a microscope in Washington, DC — at the White House.

Now I must tell you, I was not a big fan of Hillary Clinton prior to reading her book. They say she received an $8 million US advance and that the New York publishers needed to sell one million copies to break even. At this writing they have sold over 1.3 million copies at $30 per book. That is gross dollars of 39 million. I think they did OK.

The book is a long one at 585 pages, and after finishing the weighty tome, I grew to admire this highly intellectual woman for her stand on women's rights, her ability to withstand massive criticism from the press and her relentless faithfulness to her husband even after being hurt and deceived many times. Perhaps she really meant what she said in her wedding vows, "Until death do us part, in good times and in bad."

In every book I read (and I try to read one book per week) or speech that I hear, if I can take just one thing, one point, one story, one illustration, one quote or one idea home with me that could influence my life, then the exercise is not in vain.

In Hillary's book, *Living History,* I had to wade all the way through to page 505 to find it, but there it was. As the story goes, when Hillary was contemplating running for the Senate seat in New York to become that state's next senator she just couldn't make up her mind. Even her friends were giving her mixed signals.

Then she received a letter from a friend, Father George Tribou, who had run the Catholic Boys School in Little Rock for many years.

He wrote Hillary a letter dated June 24, 1999:

"Dear Hillary,

"I want to tell you what I have been telling students for 50 years: It is my opinion that on Judgment Day the first question God asks is not about The Ten Commandments (although he gets to them later), but what he asks each one of us is this: 'WHAT DID YOU DO WITH THE TIME AND THE TALENTS I GAVE YOU?'

"BOTTOM LINE: RUN, HILLARY, RUN!!"

Well, the rest is history. She ran and she won. In the process, I think Hillary found another purpose and she decided to live it on her runway of life.

Of course, not everyone is comfortable with the idea of purpose; some people prefer to say they have passion in their life, but to me it is essentially the same thing. However, passion or purpose should not be mistaken for goals; they are not the same thing. It is quite possible to have goals without a purpose. Lots of people do.

Passion and purpose are much grander things; both are connected to making a contribution in some way, to discovering the talents we were given, developing them and employing them well. A string of attained goals doesn't amount to very much in the larger scheme of things if there is no passion or purpose behind it.

The philosopher Joseph Campbell once said, "If you follow your bliss, you put yourself on a kind of track that has been there all the while, waiting for you, and the life that you ought to be living is the one you are living. When you can see that, you begin to meet people who are in your field of bliss, and they open doors to you. I say, follow your bliss and don't be afraid, and doors will open where you didn't know they were going to be."

Unfortunately, many people have never experienced that feeling of being plugged into the world around them. Instead, they get up every morning and go through the motions, feeling tired, frustrated and even resentful about the work they do every day.

William Bridges, author of *Managing Transitions,* says, "Nothing less than finding what you were meant to be and do will give you the motivation and the capability that today's work world demands. Identifying your life work is no longer an escapist fantasy. It is a condition of being successful."

So, let's get started. Small steps taken today can lead to big changes tomorrow. Here are five steps to get you on the way to finding your purpose:

1. Get a Grip on Your Fear

We all know that fear has its place, but it shouldn't stand in the way of finding your purpose. In her book *Feel the Fear and Do It Anyway,* Susan Jeffers says, "IT is what scares you

— and, ultimately, what's holding you back from going after your dream. Let's face it; shaking up your life IS scary. So go ahead and indulge in your worst-case fantasy. Then get busy figuring out what steps you can take to prevent it from happening."

2. Get Real

You've seen the ads for easy-money jobs, "Earn $1,000 a week stuffing envelopes in the comfort of your own home." Sounds great, right? Well, as my mentor Joe Segal often says, "There's no free lunch, even when someone else is buying." So, snap out of it! Finding your purpose, like everything else worthwhile, takes time and effort. A good place to start is by acknowledging the good things you already have in your life and then building on those strengths.

3. Get Involved

You have probably racked your brain trying to figure out what your ideal career is. But chances are, you've never even heard of the type of work that would be a perfect fit for you. In fact, many people who follow their passion find that it leads them into uncharted territory and eventually they 'invent' a career that is custom-fit to them. Let your natural curiosity guide you and look for ideas in the 'world' of your interests. Make it a point to simply do things you like, without trying so hard to figure out how they could turn into a career. This process will also bring you in contact with others who share your passion.

4. Get Focused

Instead of focusing on what you DON'T want — meaningless work, office politics, someone else calling the shots — zoom in on the life you DO want. Five minutes a day spent visualizing your ideal work-life and fashioning a plan to get there will move you far closer to your goal than 30 minutes of complaining.

5. Get a New Perspective

Family aside, nobody knows you better than your friends and close associates. Put together a questionnaire and send it out via email to at least 10 people you know. You can pose such questions as:

What do you think I am good at?

Do you notice any natural talents in me that you think I could develop into a career?

How am I getting in my own way, when it comes to the ideal job search?

Within a few days, you should have enough feedback to discover some trends — for example, you may notice the majority of your friends think you would be a great event organizer even if you take your planning skills for granted — and at the very least, you will have some objective ideas about your strengths and any behaviour that may be holding you back.

CHAPTER 7

What's in a Name?

When I graduated from Lester Pearson High School in New Westminster, British Columbia, I went to work for one of the oldest newspapers in this province — *The Columbian Newspaper*.

The day John F. Kennedy was assassinated I was a cub reporter and my job that day, prior to press time, was running a proof of the dramatic headline between the composing room and the publisher. Although our deadline was drawing nearer, information coming from Dallas in the aftermath of the shooting was inconsistent and confused. Was J.F.K. just shot or was he in fact dead?

The initial headlines for that day's publication read:

J.F.K. Shot

President Wounded

Sniper Shoots President

Murder in Dallas

Nation Mourns a President

Finally, minutes before the mighty presses rolled, the publisher settled on this headline:

John F. Kennedy Assassinated

I asked my boss why he chose this headline over all of the others. His answer: "His name is the most important part." I never forgot that.

How important is a name? Your name is everything! It's the link between all of the successes of your past and your future potential. You spend your lifetime protecting, enhancing and developing your name. It is you, and much of your time should be spent developing your character because that is what your name stands for.

Now in the speaking business our name is our calling card. Most of our engagements and referrals are based on our name and how the client responds when our name surfaces for a speaking opportunity.

It is true that most of us will never be celebrity speakers; therefore, we need to be the best journeyman speakers that we can be. We need to be value priced — a price that matches our ability, experience and knowledge — and remember that we can't be all things to all audiences.

If you have ever heard me speak to speakers, I almost always say, "Don't worry about the demo video, fancy brochures, professional pictures, tapes, books and all the trappings. They will come sooner than you think. Concentrate on developing your skills to be a great speaker."

In my experience, great speakers are also great storytellers. Not only do they have the facts to back up their speech, they go the extra mile to make it personal by adding stories that are sometimes funny, but always interesting, thought-provoking and have a point.

A great speaker incorporates aspects of his or her own life that are unique or dramatic as a means of connecting with audience members on a personal level.

My best advice to speakers: "Be passionate, exciting, on topic, and your future will be just fine." I believe that message is relevant no matter what profession you are in — and for your personal life, too. Whatever you decide to focus on along your personal runway, it should be something you believe in, something you can be accomplished at and something you are willing to commit yourself to for long-term results.

You must associate your name with quality, and remember, the very best referrals come from people who have been impressed with your performance in the past. It is a strategy that has served me well, and here is a great example.

Sometime near the end of 2003 I received a call from the business office for the City of Coquitlam where I have my home. I was invited to come down to city hall for a meeting. At that meeting, I was asked if I would be master of ceremonies at an inaugural event to kick off a new Ambassadors program for the city.

"We want to put the City of Coquitlam back on the map," the city administrator explained to me during the meeting.

"We've identified 150 citizens in the community who are high profile and frequently travel throughout the province and further abroad. Often when they travel they are asked the question 'Where are you from?' and they generally say Vancouver. We want them to say Coquitlam. We want them to become champions of their home city. So we are prepared to give each one of them a kit that they can share with business associates and people they meet."

Now, I have to tell you that I was very honoured by the fact that my city had chosen me to emcee the evening based on my reputation as a public speaker, my status as a local publisher and my work for the Variety Club telethon, but there is more to the story.

I got to talking with Coquitlam's economic development manager, Al Ordge, about the new Innovation Centre that has been built across the street from city hall in Coquitlam. The centre is a pilot project sponsored by the federal government.

"We've got a Web broadcast studio, high-speed wireless Internet access, 'smart' meeting rooms and lots of seminars and workshops on business topics," Al said to me, "but what we really need in the Innovation Centre is a library."

I asked him, "What kind of library?" and he said, "I don't know." Then I suggested, "Why not set up a library filled with books on leadership, business, motivation and entrepreneurship, so people who come to the Innovation Centre will have access to all of this great information from some of the world's leading experts that they probably couldn't find or afford in a regular bookstore. And how about this, I'll get you 1,000 books to get your library started."

At that point, the assembled city employees nearly fell off their chairs.

"Where are you going to get 1,000 books?" someone asked.

"I will invite my fellow speakers, business experts and associates to donate copies of their books to the library and I will provide the rest," I responded.

"Well, if you do that, we'll name the library after you," they said.

I am proud to be an Ambassador for the City of Coquitlam, British Columbia, and it is a great honour to have the new Peter Legge Library bear my name.

On the evening we launched the Ambassador program, the mayor of Coquitlam, Jon Kingsbury, said something that really stuck with me, "Coquitlam is probably one of the best-kept secrets in this region and it's high time that we started spreading the word about the tremendous advantages and opportunities that abound in our community."

I think this is a valuable message for all of us; first we must invest the time to develop our talents — whatever they may be — and then we must share them with the world, for that is how we will build our reputation and make "a name" for ourselves.

Here are five suggestions to help you build on the value of your name:

1. Delivery guaranteed

You may be an authority, have the proper credentials and a splashy advertising campaign, but can you follow through? Nothing spoils a reputation faster than failure to deliver, and most customers won't even give you the benefit of a complaint, they'll simply take their business elsewhere. Always deliver more than you promised, even if it means going out of your way or taking a short-term loss on a deal that is already signed.

2. Field of dreams

If you have a passion (and some valuable expertise) in a certain field of endeavour — be it business, sport or a hobby — offer to share it with others: give a talk to a high school group or community organization. You could also put together a seminar or workshop for newcomers to your industry or offer to mentor someone who is just starting out. You may just inspire someone to turn their dream into a reality.

3. Sweet smell of success

Always have a little anecdote or success story ready for when you meet someone new. That way, rather than going into a lengthy description of your business, you can share an interesting story of how you helped someone else solve a problem or achieve a goal.

4. Your Excellency

Be an ambassador, contact an organization that you admire and offer to volunteer your time or expertise to further their purpose and spread the word through your network of friends, acquaintances and associates.

5. I beg your pardon

It's a fact of life that we all mess up now and then. It's also true that it could get expensive if you have to change your name frequently to keep from tarnishing your reputation. When you do make a mistake, don't pass the buck; take responsibility for your error, apologize and then do something extraordinary to make up for the damage you've done.

This is what Westjet Airways does when they are unable to get a passenger on a flight for which they have a ticket. First of all, they apologize to the customer. Next, the airline staff pull out all of the stops to get the passenger on another flight to their destination as soon as possible. Finally, within a week or two, a travel voucher arrives in the mail to make up for the inconvenience. Now, based on this approach, what do you think the odds are that the customer will give Westjet another chance?

The truth is, in the end, if you conduct yourself with integrity and graciousness, no one will remember the mistake and you will have retained an important relationship. It is also quite possible that the customer will share the good news about their experience with others — and that, my friend, is how reputations are made.

What's in a name?

Looking back on that day as a cub reporter when I watched the presses roll with the headline, "John F. Kennedy Assassinated" and recalling the emotion that name alone was able to evoke in everyone around me, the answer to that question is simple: Everything! It is the one thing that precedes you into the world, and it is that which continues to speak for you after you have gone.

Of course, not everyone is going to become a famous politician or even have a library named after them. It matters not. This is your runway and the direction it takes is completely up to you. Remember, you don't develop a reputation overnight, it must be cultivated. In all of your dealings, both business and personal, ask yourself, "How will my behaviour today affect the way people will think about me tomorrow?"

CHAPTER 8

Happiness is Your Own Hot Dog Stand

Perhaps we are all entrepreneurs at heart. We have dreams of being our own boss, calling all our own shots and ultimately being the architect of a hugely successful enterprise. I can't believe if you have read this far that you have ever dreamed of making it small.

And while nearly every entrepreneur has visions of grandeur, the reality is that most businesses start out as small family operations. My first business was no different.

In fact, my very first entrepreneurial enterprise was a concession stand at the Pacific National Exhibition — a fair that runs in the city of Vancouver for about 17 days in the late summer.

At the time, I already had a full-time job at *The Columbian Newspaper* in New Westminster, but I wanted to purchase a second car for my wife. The problem was, at my current earning capacity at the newspaper, a car for Kay seemed many years away.

Enter the business opportunity. Some associates of mine were selling a concession stand that they had run at the PNE the previous year. It was called "Bunny's Foot Long Hot Dogs." At the time, foot-long hot dogs were all the rage and from the financials they showed me, it seemed a very easy 17-day venture that would enable me to buy that second car.

For a modest amount, I purchased the hot dog stand and became the proud owner of my very first venture. And that's where the problems started, problems that I hadn't even begun to think about before I handed over the money. For starters, I had no idea who was going to manage this little enterprise. I also didn't know where we were going to find suppliers or how much it would cost for stock. There was also the question of where would we get the staff to run the stand from morning to night. And what about contract negotiations with the fair?

We eventually decided that my wife would be the one to run the stand, and I know YOU saw this coming, but at the time — with visions of easy money in my head — I didn't; that created the biggest problem of all: how was my wife going to get to work? She didn't have a car.

As it turned out, we had to buy the car before we had sold one hot dog; so much for planning ahead. We settled on an Austin 1100, which cost somewhere in the neighbourhood of $475 — believe me, it seemed like a great deal of money at the time. The kicker was, we had to pay cash for the car because we hadn't yet established a good credit rating.

In the end, my Mom, Dad and I worked alongside my wife for 17 days straight from 10 a.m. to midnight. And because we couldn't afford a babysitter either, Kay brought our young daughter Samantha with her every day to work.

I think Samantha must have eaten our profits. When the 17 days were over and the smell of grilled hot dogs had finally been washed out of our clothes, we barely broke even because it rained every single day of the fair, but Kay got her car and I was happy to go back to my job at the paper . . . at least until the next entrepreneurial idea hit.

What I learned from that summer selling hot dogs in the rain is that we shouldn't be afraid to try a new venture because the only way we are going to develop the skills necessary to run a business is by actually doing it. Just like everything else along the runway of life, we learn by doing.

Of course, it is inevitable that we will make mistakes along the way, but hopefully we will learn from those mistakes and they will make us stronger and wiser — failure is an event, not a person — as we get further along our runway. As you can tell from this story, I wasn't born with business smarts; just like everyone else, I had to develop them from life experience. As Brian Tracy says, "If you can learn to drive a car — one of the most difficult things to master — you can learn any business skill." But I did have the guts to try something new, to seek out an opportunity and take a chance.

Along the way, I discovered that the beauty of starting out

small is that you can learn new skills as you go along and test your ideas and theories in a somewhat controlled, safe environment. Because of my full-time job, I knew that hot dog stand wasn't going to make or break my future. I wasn't risking the mortgage money or the security of my family. At the same time, I wasn't willing to simply stick it out at my day job and wait for the years to pass until I could finally afford that second car.

I learned a great deal that summer; primarily that entrepreneurism isn't about the "perfect opportunity," it is about passion, challenge, creativity and seizing opportunities. I took the lessons I learned from this venture with me into my next, bigger business enterprise and continued to learn and grow.

I would like to share some of those lessons with you:

Many people will tell you what you can't do; they won't tell you what you can do

The world is full of critics. More often than not, people who spend their time telling others what can't be done are problem finders, not problem solvers. They would rather be spectators than active participants in the game of life. Likewise, most times the people who have accomplished something significant in their own life are the first to encourage you to do the same. These are the people to seek out for guidance and advice on your endeavours.

Don't follow the leader, be the leader

One of my three mentors, Mel Cooper, told me, "If you serve customers with creativity, competence and commitment, the competition may catch on, but they will never catch up." If you truly want to be an entrepreneur, you must look for opportunity in situations where others see only obstacles and strike out in your own direction.

When you achieve a goal once thought unattainable, you provide the impetus for others to dream bigger, work harder and go further. For example, Roger Bannister was the first to break the four-minute mile when many said it could not be done. Today, the four-minute mile is standard in competition, simply because he proved that it *could* be done.

There is a time for daring and a time for caution; as an entrepreneur, you must know the difference

It goes without saying that all entrepreneurs make mistakes along the way. They are risk-takers, willing to do things differently in order to develop new and better solutions. That said, taking unnecessary risks is not a requirement for success; in fact, it can often be detrimental to a new venture. In truth, successful entrepreneurs are risk-minimizers, they take risks from necessity because it comes with the territory. In business as in life, a little common sense — and a practical plan — goes a long way. The motto of one of the minor Chinese monkey gods sums it up well, "Be cautious, be bold"; the two work well hand in hand.

Look at life from different perspectives and you will see what others cannot

As an entrepreneur, you don't have the resources of a big corporation, but neither do you have the restrictions. Make the most of this! Successful entrepreneurs try to look at situations or problems from many different — and often unconventional — angles and then come up with creative solutions.

Tune in to your intuition

One of the greatest gifts an entrepreneur possesses is the ability to sense what is trying to be born in the world and the courage to act on that knowing. Now when I say "sense" I am really talking about instinct rather than analytical ability. The legendary hockey player Wayne Gretzky has this sense and he explains it this way, "I skate to where I think the puck will be." It is an ability that is developed through precise observation of the environment through not just your own eyes, but those of customers, other players, competitors and even critics.

Expect resistance and learn to push through it

Entrepreneurs are constantly challenging the world to accept new ideas and using these ideas to improve society. In essence, they are out to change the world. For most people, that is a scary proposition. To succeed, you must be ready to answer this resistance and respond by demonstrating the value of your ideas again and again.

Carpe Diem

If you've seen the movie *Dead Poets Society*, you'll be familiar with this lesson. In the movie, as a teacher at an exclusive boy's school in the U.S., Mr. Keating tells his students, "Don't wait until it's too late to realize your potential. Carpe Diem — Seize the Day! To know you have lived with meaning, to know you have existed with purpose, and to know you brought life to your passions . . . then you can say, 'yes, I seized the day.'"

CHAPTER 9

Snake Charmers

If you look long and hard enough into my curriculum vitae you will discover that at one stage in my life I lived in London, England, where I was trying my hand as a professional stand-up comedian.

My interest in performing actually caught fire when I was in high school, where I had the opportunity to emcee pep rallies and school shows. It was there that I discovered not only did I have a sense of humour people appreciated, I could also connect with an audience, and that was a powerful feeling indeed.

Not long after high school I auditioned and landed a gig as master of ceremonies on a P&O cruise ship. Mind you, what they called a cruise ship back then is nothing as lavish as the floating hotels you find plying the waters today. But it was to be my first international trip and I was thrilled to be making money doing something I considered to be fun. In fact, I was so over the moon about the idea, that when the talent manager asked me where I wanted to go, I said, "I really don't care."

I ended up on the *SS Oriana*. It was a 38-day voyage from Vancouver to our destination, London, England. Upon arrival, I decided to stay in England for a while and see where life would take me. With no connections and no prospects for work, I knew that I would have to take a risk and dare to do something different to get some work. At the time, I didn't know what that was going to be, but I would soon find out.

My wife Kay and I settled in a small house in Putney where the fellow next door — his name was Peter Therry — just happened to be an independent TV producer.

After more than a few conversations over the garden wall about my aspirations as a performer, Peter managed to convince me to write a 15-minute TV show, which he produced at no charge.

That became my demo tape. As a next step, I invited about 10 producers from BBC, ITV and other British television stations to a screening of the show at an independent studio in downtown London in the hopes that they would consider a new face on TV, in particular, my face.

Among them was John Ammonds, producer of the number one comedy variety show on BBC called *Morecomb and Wise.*

He liked what he saw and before I knew it, I was in a taxi with Mr. Ammonds, headed back to his BBC office. It was during that taxi ride that we came up with the concept for a new show.

The show, titled *Don't Ask Us, We're New Here,* featured five new performers, including myself. It ran for nine weeks on BBC and at the end of its run, had an audience of nine million viewers.

Following the TV show I was booked as a headliner by my London agent on a seven-week tour of what was then known as the Bailey Circuit, mostly made up of big nightclubs in the Birmingham, Leicester, Manchester area. Based on the popularity of the TV show, I thought I had a reasonable chance of success as a comedian working many of the clubs in England and Wales.

The tradition was that you opened on a Sunday night in the city you were booked in, did one show on Sunday and two shows per night Monday through Saturday. On Sunday you would travel to your next city.

The first week I was booked into a nightclub in the Bull Ring Shopping Centre in the middle of Birmingham. I arrived at the nightclub for the sound check and rehearsal prior to checking into my digs, which were in the British equivalent to a low-priced hotel for travelling entertainers.

Immediately following the full dress rehearsal with the orchestra and the compere (master of ceremonies) for the evening I asked the nightclub manager who else was on the bill. He told me a young, attractive female singer and then pointing over to an elderly couple, sitting in a dimly lit part of the nightclub, he said, "Those two people as well."

I asked him what they did and he said, "They are snake

charmers." I said, "What do you mean? Real snakes?" He said, "Yes, including live pythons and lizards."

In my weirdest dreams I couldn't have imagined working with snake charmers and all of their reptiles for one night, let alone a whole week.

As I gazed across the room to where they were sitting, I saw myself as a 60-year-old performer struggling to make a living in the dimly lit nightclub in Birmingham. There I would be, after all those years on the road, still trying to make it in show business, the third act on the bill . . . . All of a sudden, the light went on and I could see this was not the business for me.

At that precise moment, I could feel my once-big dream of being a nightclub comic begin to die and I knew that this was a major turning point on my runway of life.

I drove to a Kentucky Fried Chicken outlet on the outskirts of Birmingham and ordered a single meal with a soft drink. As I sat looking out the window of that small take-out restaurant, eating my food, my gaze settled on one of those world-famous red English telephone boxes. I knew what I had to do. I rushed outside and telephoned my wife Kay and said to her, "Please don't challenge me on what I am about to say, but I am giving up show business and I will be back in London in three hours to explain everything."

I then committed the most unpardonable sin of any performer. I phoned the nightclub manager at the Bull Ring Shopping Centre and told him, "I can't go on tonight." He couldn't believe what he was hearing and said, "But you're the headliner. We only hired you because of your hit television show on BBC. What am I going to do? Couldn't you just perform tonight and we will get a replacement for the rest of the week?"

I said, "I am really sorry but no, my mind is made up."

As I look back on that decision now, although I know it was the right decision — I could never be a full-time stand-up comic — the implementation was clearly wrong. In my haste to change course, I displayed a definite lack of professionalism.

That was 35 years ago.

Shortly after deciding that a life of comedy was not for me, I flew back to Canada where I decided to return to my roots and pursue a career in business.

Little did I know at the time that my experiences on the comedy circuit in England were preparing me for my future on stage as a motivational speaker. I believe that experience gives me an advantage over other speakers. In public speaking as in comedy, it's all about timing. When I used to perform with the Mills brothers, all of the reviews I received said, "His timing is flawless."

And now, all these years later, it is as if I have come full circle. Although I knew when I stood on that stage in Birmingham that I had a talent, and talent is a gift to be used, I realized that my talent had not yet found the right outlet. Sometimes we pick up skills, not knowing when or how we will use them along our runway.

What this tells us is that we should not be afraid to pursue any of our dreams. For even though they don't always lead us where we expect them to — in fact, they may lead us to a place we had never imagined — they may just lead us to the place where we were meant to be. Of course, the other side of this equation is that we should always keep in mind that time is short. There is no time to waste on the runway of life. That is why when we realize we are going in the wrong direction, we need to have the courage to put on the brakes and change course.

My career as a motivational speaker (and author) is one of the most challenging and rewarding aspects of my life. It provides me with an opportunity to constantly challenge both my actions and my beliefs to make sure they are aligned with my purpose. I get an enormous amount of satisfaction from knowing that in addition to entertaining my audiences and perhaps making them laugh, I am also inspiring them to explore, expand and exploit the opportunities on their own runway. Looking back, I am amazed to think that the path to finding my true calling started with my saying no.

As an aside, I want to tell you a little story about what happened when I arrived in Vancouver, stone broke, without any prospects for a job.

On my first day back, I walked into the Bank of Nova Scotia at 10th and Langley in Burnaby and asked the manager of the bank to loan me $1,500 so that I could afford to bring my wife and our new baby daughter home from England. At this, the bank manager leaned back and took a moment to look me up and down, before inquiring, "Do you have a job, young man?"

"No," I replied.

"Well, do you have an account with this bank?" he asked.

"No," I responded, "but if you loan me the money, I will repay you."

At which point, the manager once again sat back in his chair, looking at me carefully, but saying nothing. I had no idea what was going through his head at that moment; whether he was deciding if he should show me the door or if he was just calculating the interest on the loan.

At the end of the day, the bank manager loaned me the money based on my word that I would repay him, and that is one reason why 35 years later, I still have an account at that bank. Here was a man who knew the importance of trusting his own instincts, and although I didn't have anything more than my word to offer at the time, his instinct about me turned out to be right on the money . . . it also turned out to be a very profitable relationship for his bank.

CHAPTER 10

Reading for Success

I am an unashamedly big fan of fellow Canadian Brian Tracy. Brian was born in Canada but now lives in San Diego with his wife Barbara and four children. He is considered by many people to be the world's foremost professional speaker and trainer, and he is the author of *Focal Point*; *Change Your Thinking, Change Your Life*; *Goals*; and many other best-selling motivational books.

In fact, it was Brian Tracy who first called me with an invitation to join the prestigious Speakers Roundtable comprising 20 of the world's best speakers. Needless to say, I was humbled to be thought of in this light, let alone being invited to join them.

Brian has devoted his life to reading, listening, studying and researching the qualities that make up the ingredients of a successful life both in a professional capacity and personally on the home front. He has written 26 best-selling books on this subject and recorded countless audio programs including

Psychology of Success.

I am among the legions of fans that are continually inspired by his succinct and clear way of expressing the thoughts of the countless successful giants that have gone before all of us, from Plato and Socrates, to W. Clement Stone, Napoleon Hill and Zig Ziglar.

Brian has distilled the very best wisdom from the ages and modernized it so that we might apply these important principles to our lives and enjoy the advantages and successes that we all want.

Brian's approach to success is a valid one. That's why reading is so important. Reading opens us up to new worlds, adventures and ideas. It broadens our thinking and our vocabulary. Most of all, it inspires us to dream.

I have heard it said that, "Nobody dreams of making it small." No one can tell you how far you can go, it is up to you.

As I've quoted Denis Waitley's words before, "We are all born with the seeds of greatness."

I believe that to be true, those seeds need to be nurtured, fertilized and developed to grow in our lives over a long period of time so that on this runway of life we accomplish all that we are able to and leave nothing on the table when our runway runs out. We can fertilize our minds with the thoughts and ideas that come from good books.

For those of you who have read more than one of my previous books, you will notice that I often talk about the importance of reading. Personally, I make a point to read at least one book per week. That adds up to more than 50 books a year.

Although a book a week may seem like a lot of reading, let's be clear that I'm not talking about browsing, skimming or speed reading. Good books deserve to be read slowly, deliberately and repeatedly. Between reading sessions, spend some time thinking about how these ideas relate to your situation. Remember, new thoughts and ideas are of no use if you choose not to apply them in your life.

Many people will read an enlightening book or attend a motivating seminar that inflates them with confidence and direction only to have the excitement and glow wear off after a few days because they don't follow through. That is why it is so important to read, reread and apply.

Think of it this way, ideas are the tools you will use to build the life you dream about. Once you have acquired some good tools, make a commitment to yourself to use them regularly. With application comes a deeper sense of understanding that will lead you to success sooner.

Of course, using knowledge is not just the purpose of your learning; it is the very basis of the learning process. In his book, *How to Study*, Arthur Kornhauser, an associate professor of business psychology at the University of Chicago, wrote, "Knowledge is acquired only through thinking and doing . . . Learning is an active process. Use your knowledge by thinking, talking and writing about the things you are learning."

Next to following through, one of the biggest mistakes people make in regards to reading is to put a book down when they come to an idea they don't agree with. No one says that each situation will apply to you or that you have to agree with the author at every turn.

Many of the best articles and books about success have been written for a sales or business audience. That doesn't mean that just because you are not involved in running a business you should ignore them. These books often contain principles and techniques that can be applied to many aspects of life. Simply be willing to explore other ways of thinking and then take what you can use from each book.

Here are some more tips on making the most of your reading for success:

Coffee talk

Discuss and share ideas with others. Talk about what you have learned with friends and family. Even if you end up in the odd debate, you will be using what you learn.

Name a library after . . . You

Build your own success library. Collect books and clip out articles that inspire you and review them whenever you need a little inspiration or motivation in your life.

Share the wealth . . . and the wisdom

Send articles to friends and business associates. When you find topical information that you think might help someone else, don't hesitate to pass it along. We could all use a little boost now and then in terms of new ideas. It's also a great way to motivate staff members or give a friend or family member some extra encouragement.

Thirty minutes a day could change your life

Read something useful, challenging or educational every day. Thirty minutes spent with a book that motivates, excites and educates you will make a world of difference. My Speakers Roundtable colleague Charlie "Tremendous" Jones said, "We will be the same person in five years except for the people we meet, the places we go and the books we read." He also challenged me with the question, "What books are you rereading?"

The world according to . . . You

Keep a journal for your thoughts and ideas and try to carry it with you. This will help you track your progress and make your learning more tangible. It is also a good place to record quotes that inspire you and list books you want to read.

The tuition is reasonable, just don't fall asleep in class

Rev up your university on wheels. Listen to educational,

motivational and entertaining tapes while you drive. Forget the bad news stations and talk radio. Fill your mind with the best information you can find and you will arrive at your destination feeling energized.

It has often been said, "Success is a journey, not a destination." It's still true. Associate reading with having fun, growing as an individual and getting closer to your dreams. Reading should be enjoyable, as well as educational.

CHAPTER 11

Learning from the Giants

As Disraeli so wisely noted, "All of us encounter, at least once in our life, some individual who utters words that make us think forever. There are men whose phrases are oracles; who can condense in one sentence the secrets of life; who blurt out an aphorism that forms a character, or illustrates an existence."

Last year Brian Tracy spoke to my entire company — all 100 of us. As I sat to attention, listening to Brian, I couldn't write fast enough to get down all of the valuable lessons he has learned from the thousands of books he has read and distilled to make him one of the richest-content business speakers in the world.

In this chapter, I want to share with you 50 principles I learned from Brian on how to change your life:

Do more of certain things that work

Life is too short to perfect your weaknesses or to struggle to make something work when your instincts tell you that it won't. It's a funny thing that so many people have been brainwashed to believe endless struggle is a good thing. Don't you think it would be more fun to work smart?

Usually, I find we have opportunities right under our noses that we aren't recognizing or taking advantage of. Just as technology companies invest in research and development, so should you. A simple assessment of where you are spending your time and where your results are coming from will help determine what is working well.

When you find yourself stuck, take a moment to look at what IS working and see if you can do more of that. Also, when you discover something that works for you, don't be afraid to run with it and possibly distill it down to a formula that can be used in other areas of your life.

Do less of other things that aren't working

Take time out on a regular basis to assess what is NOT working for you in both your business and life. This is no time for ego; if you're too proud to admit you're wrong, you'll fail by continuing to pour your efforts into things that aren't working rather than shifting them to try new things that might be more successful.

While there is pain associated with admitting something didn't work, feeling shame and assigning blame are the wrong things to do. They take up precious time and energy. The point here is to eliminate things that aren't working and move on.

Admire successful people

We all need role models; make a point to seek out successful people to admire and emulate. Choose people with goals and plans, people who are going somewhere with their lives and have high aspirations. Just be sure to choose them carefully, and remember, not all people with money are successful and not all successful people have money.

Whatever you criticize, drive it out of your life

If you dislike something enough to spend the time and energy to criticize it, make a point to push it out of your life to ensure that it will not continue to take up future time and energy. Negative ideas and emotions require a great deal more energy than positive ones.

You become what you praise

Whatever you give attention to is what you get in your life. When you praise something, not only are you voicing your support or approval for it, you are also making room in your life for more of it. You are focusing on what is positive and constructive, which means you have less time for what is negative or destructive.

Persist longer and try more things to increase your probability of success

The most often-repeated story of failure — and persistence — is Thomas Edison's tale of his 2,000 failed attempts at creating an effective light bulb before he succeeded. If Edison were alive today, experts would no doubt say that he suffered from an obsessive-compulsive disorder and recommend therapy.

It is a great benefit to the world that he was so persistent — we should all be such fabulous failures — and eventually . . . successful. If you apply that same kind of persistence in your own life, in the long run, there is absolutely no way you can fail.

Expect to be successful

See yourself as the very best in your field. Remember, all improvement in your life begins with an improvement in your mental pictures. Visualize yourself; see yourself as the best continually. You are the best. Isn't that right? So, see yourself as the best.

Be optimistic

On the path to becoming the person you want to be, you must be prepared for both obstacles and opportunities by remaining imaginatively flexible and optimistically open to new and unexpected ways of achieving your goals. For almost every major challenge you will face, the key to success lies in how you make up your mind to approach the situation. Ask yourself, "Is it just an obstacle, or is it perhaps an opportunity disguised as an obstacle?"

The results you get determine the balance of your life

It doesn't matter where you are coming from — all that matters is where you are going. You may have gotten where you are today largely by accident, but where you are headed in the future is completely up to you — be the architect of your own transformation.

You become what you feed into your mind

In the same way that your body requires healthy food, exercise and a reasonable amount of sleep to thrive, your mind also requires regular nourishment, exercise and rest. Choose to read books that motivate, inspire and make you think.

Positive thoughts reap positive results. You'll attract more people and business when you're feeling good and projecting positive energy. Also, make sure that you are getting enough time off and rest to balance the focused time you spend developing your mind. You need to be at your sharpest and your best.

The more you like yourself, the more you will do things well — the better you do, the more you will like yourself

This sounds a lot like the "Which came first, the chicken or the egg?" paradox, but you don't have to sit around waiting for something to hatch. Simply get started and do more. The more you do, the more competent you will become and the more confidence you will have in yourself. The more confidence you have, the more you will like yourself. The more you like yourself, the higher your self-esteem. The higher your self-esteem is, the greater your self-discipline. The more self-discipline you have, the more you will persist . . . and that, ultimately, will make you unstoppable.

Learn from the experts, do what successful people do

There's a saying in coaching circles: "Sometimes you have to fake it until you make it." Simply put, it means if you want to be successful — and the habits you have are not getting the results you want — look closely at the habits of people you admire and emulate those habits in your own life.

Thoughts are causes, conditions are effects

On average, a person has 60,000 separate thoughts a day. Every thought you have either makes you stronger or weaker. Thoughts of kindness, forgiveness and peace are strengthening. Focusing on anger, anxiety and worry weaken you. If you keep your 'creating attention' focused on the outlook that the universe is plentiful and providing, you'll attract abundance and support. If you dwell on the view that you're being short-changed and nothing ever goes right, you'll experience a world of scarcity and struggle.

All unhappiness is blame, stop blaming

Get rid of energy drains. Resolve any issues that you have been brooding about for a long time. Bury the hatchet with friends and relatives. Praise people rather than criticize. Detach from the need to be right — and from the habit of judging or controlling others. Catch yourself verbalizing self-defeating thoughts.

Think about what you want, most people think about what they don't want

Remember when you were young, lying on your back in the grass watching the clouds go by, daydreaming about all the things you would do when you grew up? Remember too, how those daydreams filled you with a sense of anticipation and optimism? When did you stop doing that?

Never forget that you have the creative power to accomplish the deepest desires of your heart. And what's more, you can never be truly happy as long as you deny your innermost dreams. So take the time to think deeply on what you want in your life and to map out your dreams on paper. Be bold and imaginative.

Your outer world becomes your inner world

We are all strongly influenced by the people, thoughts and atmosphere around us. We absorb the energy of what we allow into our space. Whatever we surround ourselves with, that is what we are choosing to give power in our lives. This is especially true when we stay stuck in a job that we hate or find ourselves surrounded by people who are negative or argumentative.

Instead, why not choose to be with people who have the same life focus as you; cut short draining conversations; give extra time to interactions that are exhilarating and switch to more inspirational reading that activates the best aspects of your character.

People who are optimistic live longer

A 30-year patient study done by the Mayo Clinic proved it. According to Dr. Toshihiko Maruta, M.D., a Mayo Clinic psychiatrist and lead author of the study, "It confirmed our common-sense belief. It tells us that mind and body are linked and that attitude has an impact on the final outcome, death."

In an editorial that accompanied publication of the study in February 2000, Martin E.P. Seligman, Ph.D., of the Department of Psychology at the University of Pennsylvania, wrote, "Pessimism is identifiable early in life and changeable. So it is possible that individuals at specific physical risk might . . . change their thinking about bad events and so lower their risk for physical illness and even death."

You have more potential than you can use in a lifetime

For most of us, when our endeavours don't turn out quite the way we expected, we become discouraged and lose all sense of perspective about our talent or potential. It's not that we lack potential, more often it is because we are too close to "the problem" or don't know how to get started in a new direction.

If you don't know where your potential lies, get a buddy or a coach. Whether you choose a formal coaching relationship or ask an associate to be your accountability partner, having someone to bounce ideas off of, to share your dreams and vision with and to give you a kick in the rear when you need it can make the difference between being ordinary and being extraordinary.

Eighty per cent of people's energy is used on worry about facts — you can't change facts — the past is a fact

It is time to put your focus on the present. As much as we can't control or predict the future or other people's behaviours, we also cannot change what has happened in the past. All we can control is our own actions, right here, right now.

As the phrase on the T-shirt says, "Learn from the past and then get the hell out of there!"

Wealthy people watch TV in another room, poor people watch TV in the dining room

You choose. Which one do you want to be?

Create new habits

To unlock your inner potential, you must set very clear, challenging and yet realistic goals and then make specific plans to accomplish them. You need to work, step by step, every day, in the direction of your dominant aspirations. Often, that involves developing new, more productive habits. As you come up with new habits to replace old ones, write them down and practice them on a daily basis. Remember, it takes about three weeks for a new habit to take hold, so don't get discouraged and don't give up.

Get rid of three white poisons in your diet — sugar, flour, salt — replace them with fruits and vegetables

You need a healthy body to go with the fabulous life you are creating for yourself. Replacing these three refined foods with whole, natural fruits and vegetables will give you energy and a boost of the vitamins and minerals your body craves. Remember, for best results, whenever you are getting rid of an old habit that was bad for you, you should always replace it with a new one that is healthy to eliminate that feeling of "something is missing" — this is a great place to start!

Make a dream list, imagine no limitations

You must decide what's right for you, what will make you happiest, before you decide what's possible. You must set ideal standards and goals and results as your aim and then determine how to accomplish them.

Don't talk yourself out of something you really want to do simply because it may not seem practical, or you're worried about what others may think, or you feel it's too late. Often the most practical thing you can do is to be true to yourself and vigorously explore the path of your dreams.

The more clear you are about your future, the better off you will be

Write down all the things that are important to you (include possessions, people and feelings). Then write out what you want to contribute to the world. From your writing, create a statement of purpose for yourself that you can read each and every day.

Future intent determines present action

In his book *The Path of Least Resistance*, Robert Fritz calls this your "future vision." The clearer you are about your ideal result or future vision, the easier it is for you to alter your actions and behaviours in the short term to assure that you get where you want to be in the long term. Once you've clearly decided on the person you would like to become, you are on the path toward developing new beliefs. You then discipline yourself each day to behave exactly as you would if you were already that person.

The act of deciding what you want increases the chance of your getting it by 100 per cent

By simply deciding what you want, you rule out all other possibilities and allow all of your energy to flow to that one purpose. Then, each time you think about or refine it, the imprint of your purpose goes deeper into your being and your probability of success increases as your attention becomes intensely focused on one thing.

Do something every day on your master goal

In the words of Mark Twain, "The secret of getting ahead is getting started." Although your master goal may be a big one, the secret of getting started is breaking your complex overwhelming tasks into small manageable tasks and then starting on the first one.

In the end, the little things can add up to make a big difference, so take time to work on at least one aspect of your goal every day. Instead of wasting a small window of time, use it to take a forward action. Even 10 minutes a day can make a difference in your end result and you'll be surprised at how 10 minutes a day adds up over time — that's almost an hour of any given work week or 52 hours in a year.

Successful people are results oriented

It's a fact of life that you can only achieve by doing. It doesn't matter what you say or what you wish, hope, dream or intend to do. If you don't do it, it doesn't matter. Actions get results and results determine success.

What can I — and only I — do that done well will make a difference

In business and in life, developing a niche is an important way to distinguish yourself from the masses and make an impact on others. It's a fact, when we want something done, we want it done right, that's why we are much more likely to seek out — and pay — a specialist or "expert."

Take action, develop a sense of urgency

Have you ever noticed that when you actually get down to business and take action on a task that help starts to flow to you from areas you haven't even focused on? You're taking care of things in your sphere of influence and all of a sudden the perfect opportunity to further your project just materializes from an outside source.

The common conception is that motivation leads to action, but the reverse is actually true — action comes before motivation. You have to prime the pump and get things flowing before you will gain the momentum that will motivate you to work on your goals. Getting momentum going is the most difficult part of the job, and often taking the first step is enough to prompt you to make the best of your day.

#1 Focus, and #2 Concentration, don't guarantee success, but lack of both determines failure

Having the capacity to focus on a goal is like finding the right path through the woods. Concentration is the ability to remain clear, purposeful and directed enough to follow the path and come out the other side at your destination. Both are abilities that can be developed through practice.

Most people spend only 20 to 30 per cent of their time on the specific actions that will lead to achieving their desired goals. That means up to 80 per cent of their time is taken up by activities that are not contributing to their goals. That leaves a great deal of room for improvement.

Work all the time you are at work — just because you are at work doesn't mean you are working — if you go off course, say to yourself, "Back to work"

Every job that you undertake deserves your best effort. If you are just wasting time at work, rethink your career choice. After all, you're not just wasting your time, you're also wasting your potential and robbing yourself of the feeling of satisfaction that comes with a job well done. Also, if you want to move ahead, remember to take some time every week to work ON your business, not just work in it.

If you are in sales and want to double your income, double your prospecting

If you want more, the bottom line is, you have to do more — end of story!

Luck is based on probability

It seems like luck, but it's the old saying about the more prepared you are, the luckier you get. You can increase your luck by doing your homework. That means researching and learning everything you can about what you want to accomplish and then going and applying what you learned.

Everything you do counts

The choices you make determine the life that you have. It may not seem like it, but each and every day, the small actions that you take accumulate and create a pattern in your life. With everything that you do, be mindful of the pattern you are creating with your actions.

In the fullness of time, 70 per cent of your decisions are wrong

Sounds a little grim at first blush, but it's actually a pretty good average. In baseball, if you walk up to the plate and fail to get on base 70 per cent of the time, they call you a hero. So why is it so hard to understand that batting 300 and making your best effort every time is the secret to success in life?

You just have to keep trying lots of things, keeping track of what's working and what's not, and then running with the things that work. If you're too afraid to take your lumps, you'll fail by never having found your next great success. If you're too arrogant to admit when you're wrong, you'll fail by pouring your efforts into things that aren't working rather than shifting them to things that may.

One way to improve your batting average is to pull back and examine the assumptions upon which you are basing your strategy to determine whether or not they are still valid. Think of it as calling a "time-out."

If you succeed, you do it again

No need to reinvent the wheel every time you want to go for a spin. Once you find something that works, do it again, and then again and again and again and again. Some of the most successful people in the world got where they are by relying on this very simple formula.

Take full responsibility for your life and the decisions you make

Choose to live life on your terms, not someone else's. Define success for yourself. What would it look like and feel like? Write down what success means for you. Use these answers as your barometer. Make your priority whatever is most important to you — God, family, friends, passion, art, your life purpose. You'll find that decisions come more easily, and you'll activate more support, love, money and magic in your life.

Carry no grudges — they're bad for you and they're heavy

Have you ever noticed how negative thoughts and feelings

weigh you down, while positive ones make you feel taller and lighter? That's because negative thoughts take a lot of energy and tend to be like weeds in the garden. If you let one take root, pretty soon you have a whole bunch of them filling up your mind, stealing away your energy, your happiness and sense of well-being. If you have a problem with someone, face it straight on and resolve it the best way you can, then forget about it.

Use the word "How." "How can I ——?" You fill in the blanks

It's amazing what a difference perspective makes. Once you put yourself in the frame of mind that anything is possible, it is simply a matter of determining "how."

Project yourself five years into the future in terms of health, position and income

Peter Drucker's words from the previous chapter on goals bear repeating: "We overestimate what we can do in one year, but we underestimate what we can do in five years." If you plan and project, you won't underestimate yourself.

Imagine no limitations

Most of our self-limiting beliefs have no basis whatsoever in fact. They are based on information and ideas that we have accepted as true, sometimes in early childhood, and to the degree to which we accept them as fact, they become real for us. The same is true of our unlimited potential — to the degree that we believe in it, it is ours!

Future-oriented people live much longer

Why is that? Most likely it is because they are always looking forward to something. They want the most out of life and they face the future with a sense of anticipation rather than fear.

Because a lot of people lose their focus and drive when they retire, one of the simplest ways to extend your life is to move your "best before" or retirement date a little further along the runway. Rather than retiring at 65, you should consider working to 75 years of age and then plan for about 15 years of retirement. That sounds more reasonable, don't you think?

Remember the momentum principle of success; it is the key to long-term results

We all know that it takes a lot of energy to get started. However, once you get moving in a particular direction, it takes very little energy to keep going. That's because you have the principle of momentum working in your favour. However, if you stop, it's hard to get started again.

For example, if you've come back from a vacation of a week or two, you'll notice that it takes you several days to start working at peak efficiency again. This is part of the momentum principle.

How do you use the momentum principle in your life? Well, it's simple. You decide upon one key quality that you need to develop in order to accomplish one key goal that you want to accomplish. Then every single day, you work simultaneously on developing that quality and on taking steps toward the accomplishment of that goal. Once you put the ball into play, you keep the game going every single day, without stopping.

Failure is not an option

It is true in life and in business that you often have to try different ways of approaching a problem before you find a solution that works. In that sense, solutions can be like keys; you may have to try them one by one until you find the one that opens the door. You only truly fail when you give up.

Ask yourself "Why am I on the payroll?"

Whether you are the boss or someone's employee, this is a good question. What value is your contribution making to the success of the business you work for?

The most common belief is I'm not good enough

If you don't believe in yourself, who else will? Through faith in yourself, you enable the world around you to give back to you. Through your belief in yourself, you create your world, your life, your potential. Making mistakes is part of being human and it is an essential part of the learning process.

Learn from your mistakes — they will make you stronger and wiser — and keep going.

Leaders have a vision of what they want in the future

Life is too short to work so hard at pursuits that aren't really fulfilling! You can either live your life regretting all the roads left unexplored, or you can start living the life you really want. Write your dreams down on paper to give them concrete form and power. You now have an energized blueprint of what you want and this gives your subconscious a clear signal for what to attract. To add even more voltage to your goals, visualize how you would like each day to go. Shift from thinking of yourself as a victim to realizing you can be the source, cause and creator of what happens to you.

Eliminate the words "if only" from your life

You can accomplish anything you set your mind to, but "only if" you follow this advice: "Eliminate the words 'if only' from your life, they are a dead end road." As Ernest Hemingway said, "Now is no time to think of what you do not have. Think of what you can do with what there is."

Set a deadline for your goals

Just like your intentions to clean out the garage, having a goal without a deadline is like saying to yourself, "I'll get around to it one day."

You know it's true that tasks are much more likely to get finished when they have a deadline. It works the same way for goals. Think of it as planning for success. Once you set a due date, you've made a commitment to yourself and even your subconscious will begin putting the pieces in place to make it happen.

Remember, there are only so many days on your runway of life and none of us knows for sure how many, so why not be bold and make the most of each one?

Above: That's me in the middle between two men I am proud to call my mentors. Joe Segal, who inspired this very volume, is on the left, and on the right is Mel Cooper. Left: Rosalie and Joe Segal have been married for 50 incredible years, and together have taught me much about dedication, generosity and kindness.

Left: The Garment Industry Award that I presented to Joe Segal at the Hotel Vancouver is but one of numerous honours he has received. Above: Guests Rosalie Segal and Olympic gold medallist Catriona LeMay Doan at the 2003 BCBusiness TOP 100 Dinner. Right: When Vancouver won the bid for the 2010 Winter Olympics, I celebrated at GM Place Stadium alongside Karen Baker-MacGrotty of the Royal Bank, and Graeme Stamp, 2005 chair of The Vancouver Board of Trade.

Above left: My wife Kay and I at The Vancouver Board of Trade Governor's Banquet. Left: Kay and I with Joe on his home balcony with its stunning view. Above right: With distinguished CBC president Carole Taylor and B.C. Lieutenant Governor Iona Campagnolo. Right: Outgoing chair Carole Taylor and the infamous red shoes at my induction as chair of The Vancouver Board of Trade.

Board of Trade

Top left: The three doctors — Dr. Legge, Dr. Segal and Dr. Segal — at Simon Fraser University. Left: Ruy Paes-Braga of the Four Seasons Vancouver and I presented Joe Segal with a painting of the inimitable Winston Churchill. Top right: As respective out-going and incoming Board chairs, Carole Taylor and I honoured Rosalie and Joe with the Community Leadership Award. Right: Rosalie and I in conversation at one of many dinners we've enjoyed together.

Top left: My three mentors — giants among men Ray Addington, Joe Segal and Mel Cooper. Top right: Dare to dream big! Right: The out-going chair of the Board of Trade received this treasured sculpture for his years of service.

CHAPTER 12

Love's Labour Found

I'll admit to you right now that I have never been very good with my hands. While some people can pick up a piece of wood and with just two or three tools turn it into a beautiful piece of furniture, I have not been so blessed.

When I was just 16 years old I got a summer job at Fraser Mills in Surrey, British Columbia, working the midnight to 8 a.m. shift feeding the dryer to help make sheets of plywood. It took two of us to feed this big machine.

My co-worker was 40 years old and making essentially the same money I was. After eight weeks of labouring, I decided I would never work with my hands again.

Now, I'm not telling you this story because I want to put down people who do physical jobs to earn their living. The reason I am telling you this is because it is important for each one of us to decide what we want out of life and to go with what works for us.

What I really thought to myself is that I am not going to

make much of my life working at a mill for an hourly wage. In my mind's eye I saw myself at 40 still feeding that dryer and I knew that my talents lay elsewhere. I also knew that I needed to keep trying different things until I discovered what those talents were.

In fact, if I had never set off in search of my talent I would have missed out on the most important opportunity of my life, the chance to meet my future wife, Kay.

Like me, Kay was born in England. When she was 18, Kay's father was contracted to work for Boeing in Seattle, Washington. When he left England, he took his family with him overseas. Kay ended up working at Seattle's First National Bank. However, after a year in the States, she decided to return to England.

At the same time, I had just landed my very first entertainment assignment for the cruise ship company P&O, as an emcee. I was to set sail on the *SS Oriana*, for a 38-day voyage from Vancouver to London, England.

Although I had the good fortune to be accommodated on the first-class deck of the ship, because I was an entertainer, I was instructed to have one of my meals each day in the tourist cabin. I decided that I really didn't want to get up and have breakfast there each morning and I knew the dinners would be better in first class, so I thought I would go to the tourist dining room for lunch.

As luck would have it, on the very first day at lunch, I didn't sit at my assigned table. For some reason that I can no longer remember, I chose to sit at a different table and Kay was seated next to me. To say that I was immediately smitten is an understatement, but also a tasteful description of the effect this beautiful young woman had on me, so I will stick with it. I soon discovered that she was sailing back to England to meet her fiancé and to decide whether or not she still wanted to marry him after a year apart.

During that lunch, Kay and I hit it off and soon fell head over heels in love. When we arrived in Jamaica some 30 days into the voyage, I told her, "I don't want Tony meeting you in London and I don't want you to marry him, I want you to marry me." Six months after the ship docked in England, we were married. We stayed there for about two years before returning to Canada.

I would like to share another story with you about a fellow with a very special talent, who was born just down the road from my family's home in Wales.

Most of you have heard of Tom Jones, the international singing star who had hits such as *It's Not Unusual, Delilah* and *What's New Pussycat* in the 1960s and 1970s and has since reinvented himself for younger audiences. However, it is likely that very few of you have heard of Tom Jones, the bricklayer, or "hod-carrier" as they are known in England and Wales (where Jones was born). They are called hod-carriers because as labourers, they actually carry bricks on their back.

At one point in his career, sometime after he had made it as a star, Jones was scheduled to do a production number with some back-up singers at a TV station in London, England. The previous night he had been partying and drinking heavily. So, he arrived at the station in his Rolls Royce motor car not at all in the mood to perform.

As he got out of his car he looked up and saw a labourer carrying bricks up a ladder. It so happened that the labourer knew Jones used to do the same job. He looked down at Jones and said, "Hey Tom, do ya wanna give me a hand?"

At that moment it dawned on Jones that he had no right to complain about the unique work he was doing. He had been discovered, he had a God-given talent and was getting paid handsomely to do something he loved to do. People all over the world knew his name and bought his records, women swooned when they heard him sing and men wanted to be him. In an instant, he snapped to attention, realizing just how fortunate he was and headed into the studio to do the show.

It's a lesson that Jones apparently never forgot. At the end of March 2004, Tom Jones did a show in Vancouver. At the age of 63, he was still rocking and still making the women swoon. This is what Jones had to say about his longevity, "When I was 25, if somebody said, 'You're going to be still singing as strong as ever at 60,' I'd have thought, 'Really? Is that possible?' It is possible."

I first met Tom Jones in 1969 on the set of the first Engelbert Humperdink show that was being produced at Elstree Studios just outside of London for ABC television in the U.S. Along with Jones, Barbara Eden and Jose Felliciano were also on the show.

It was meant to be Engelbert's introduction to the U.S. audience. I remember, even at that time, there were rumblings that Tom Jones was straining his voice and wouldn't last as long as Engelbert; actually, the reverse turned out to be true.

I was master of ceremonies for the production — however, in England I was a compere — and the voiceover for that show because my accent was neither American nor British, but could appeal to both audiences.

As it turned out, this show was, in fact, the very last thing I did in England before my wife and I headed back to Canada. I did the show with an option that should they pick it up, I would be the emcee. I still have the telegram I received shortly after arriving in Vancouver, telling me that ABC was picking up the show and they were offering me an eight-week contract.

Despite our paths crossing all those years ago, today, Tom Jones wouldn't know me from a bricklayer, but recently I watched him on *Larry King*. As I sat there taking in what Jones had to say as he spoke about the longevity of his career and the price of fame, it reminded me of all that I have accomplished and experienced in my own life. I look back and I marvel at what I have done.

Radio broadcaster and author Rick Forchuk once told me that most people are willing to pay the price to become successful; however, they are not willing to pay the price to stay successful. I agree. We have to keep growing as individuals, and to grow we have to use our minds.

It is interesting that the people — those who are unhappy, angry, dissatisfied or blaming of others — who would benefit most by going to seminars, reading books or advancing their education are not the ones who do so.

What about you? Is your runway of life satisfying? Do you love what you do? If so, keep on doing it the best way you know how. However, if things aren't right for you, think about what it is costing you personally to stay stuck where you are. Putting up with stuff gets you down, especially at work, where you spend more than 30 per cent of your time each week.

If you feel you are just putting in time — clock-watching and poor performance are signs of this — if you feel your talents are wasted or not recognized, why not take some time to make a list of what you like to do and what you are good at. You can also ask others for their input. Then set out on your own voyage of discovery. Something much better is out there for you and when the fit is right, you will know it.

I'd like to close this chapter with these words from dancer Martha Graham: "There is vitality, a life force, an energy, a quickening that is translated through you into action, and because there is only one of you in all of time, this expression is unique. If you block it, it will never exist through any other medium and it will be lost. The world will not have it. It is not your business to determine how good it is, nor how valuable, nor how it compares with other expressions. It is your business to keep it yours clearly and directly, to keep the channel open."

May there be abundant opportunities on the runway ahead.

CHAPTER 13

Passion

I recently heard a radio interview while I was sitting in the back of a limo heading from Toronto's Lester B. Pearson airport en route to a speaking engagement at Niagara on the Lake. At one point in the conversation, the interviewer asked the caller, "What is the difference between ignorance and apathy?" The caller responded, "I don't know and I don't care."

Although I realize the caller was going for a laugh with his comment, it got me thinking about the destructive power of the words, "I don't care." "I don't care" is a dead end road, it leaves us with nowhere to turn. If we are genuinely intent on becoming successful in life, we can't say "I don't care."

I truly believe the most important goal for each of us on our runway of life is to first discover our passion and then to live our passion. When I am talking about passion, I am not talking about a brand of perfume. I am talking about a burning drive that ignites your heart and drives you to change your world. Although it can be elusive — when was the last time you met someone who was really on fire for what he or she did? — history is full of examples of those who have succeeded in the search for their passion. It is said that all great speakers have enormous passion for their topic.

Bill Gates is perhaps one of the most palpable modern examples of how living your passion can pay off. I'm sure it is no coincidence that his company, Microsoft, has a new television commercial with the tagline "Your Potential, Our Passion."

Sam Walton built a multi-billion-dollar business on technology and business sense. He was the founder of Wal-Mart and he developed a list of 10 rules for building a business. Rule number one on Sam's list was to commit with a passion to your business. From humble beginnings in Bentonville, Arkansas, Sam built Wal-Mart into the biggest company in the world.

Jack Welch, former president of General Electric, in his book *Just Jack*, said, "Great organizations can ignite passion." According to Jack, that means nothing is held back and there are no regrets — at the end of the day, nothing is left on the table.

Of course, passion comes in many shapes and sizes. Your passion might be like that of billionaire Jimmy Pattison who owns 100 per cent of Jim Pattison Enterprises in Vancouver, Canada. Pattison's passion drove him to build a company doing $5.5 billion worth of business with 26,000 employees.

Clearly he doesn't do it for the money but for the excitement and the passion of the business.

Your passion might be like that of my youngest daughter Amanda, who from a very early age discovered she had an uncanny ability to work with children. Whenever we would go to friends' homes where there were children, in a matter of moments they were drawn to Amanda like a magnet.

Although she is the youngest of my three daughters, as a child, whenever Amanda would play school with her older sisters, she was always the teacher and they were her willing students. Amanda was still very young when she told me she wanted to be a school teacher and she never wavered from her goal. She had to graduate from two different universities to get her teaching certificate, but today she lives her passion as a grade two school teacher. I have no doubt that one day she will be teacher of the year.

Perhaps your passion will take a different course, like Amanda's husband Trevor. Several years ago, Trevor graduated from a leading Canadian university with an honours degree in business and computer science. Following university, he went to work as a management consultant. I thought that Trevor was happy enough in his career choice until he came to me one day and said, "I am not living my passion."

I asked him what his passion was and he said that he had always wanted to be a medical doctor. Now at this point in their marriage, Trevor and Amanda had a lovely 2,600-square-foot, fully furnished three-bedroom townhouse, two cars in the garage and all the trappings of a double-income newlywed couple.

So I said to Trevor, "If that's your passion, then let's make a list of what you will have to do to make it happen. First of all, you are going to have to sell your townhouse and downsize to an 800-square-foot apartment. You will also need to sell one of your cars, probably the new one. That means you will have to take public transportation. If you want to have a chance at med school, you are going to have to go back to university to take your sciences and get straight As. In addition, you will have to convince my daughter to be the breadwinner for the next four to five years and convince my daughter and my wife that there will be no grandchildren for three to four years. After all that, you are going to have to apply to every medical school in Canada in the hopes of being accepted. In other words, Trevor, you are going to have to sacrifice big time for your dream and your passion."

Guess what? He is doing just that and he expects to be applying to medical school in September 2004. That's how strong a force real passion is.

John Schappert, who is the general manager of Electronic Arts Canada — a company that claims to be the biggest entertainment company in the world specializing in software games — says that when he is looking to hire a new staff member he either:

a) hires for talent AND passion,

b) hires for talent OR passion, or he

c) doesn't hire at all.

Legendary business billionaire and host of the hit television show, *The Apprentice*, Donald J. Trump says that the key ingredient to long-lasting success is passion. In one of the magazines I receive from my speaking colleagues, *Performance Magazine*, Trump says that passion is one of the most overlooked ingredients for success.

According to Trump, passion is enthusiasm on a grand scale. He goes on to say that passion is far reaching, all encompassing, tenacious and sometimes even larger than life, and that people with passion never give up because they never have a reason to give up. Those with passion, he says, no matter what their circumstances may be, have an intangible momentum that can make them indomitable. Bottom line — when you are faced with a tough decision between two candidates — always hire passion over talent.

In 2003 I was chair of The Vancouver Board of Trade and spent some time working on the Vancouver Whistler 2010 Olympic Bid. We invited Governor Leavitt of the State of Utah to come to Vancouver and address a 700-person symposium on the value of the 2002 Olympics to his state.

In his presentation, Leavitt used the closing song of the Winter Olympics in Salt Lake City, Utah, which goes like this:

Life can be a challenge
Life can seem to be impossible
It's never easy
When there is so much on the line.

But you can make a difference
There's a mission just for you
Just look inside and you will find
Just what you can do!

That's the key, isn't it? To find out just what you can do. As Ralph Waldo Emerson once said, "What lies behind you and what lies before you pales in comparison to what lies within you." I believe if we look inside, we will find our passion and then we must start living our passion and incredible opportunities will open for us.

In the question period following his presentation at The Board of Trade, a reporter asked Leavitt, "Knowing what you do now, would you do it all again?" His answer: "In a heartbeat."

Dr. Benjamin E. Mays, the late president of Morehouse College near Atlanta, once said:

It must be borne in mind
That the tragedy in life
Does not lie in not reaching your goal
The tragedy in life is having no goal to reach.
It is not a calamity to die with dreams unfulfilled
But it is a calamity not to dream.
It is not a disaster to be unable to capture your ideal
But it is a disaster to have no ideal to capture.

It is not a disgrace not to reach the stars
But it is a disgrace to have no stars to reach for.

Some people are passionate for 30 seconds, some people are passionate for 30 minutes, some people are passionate for 30 days, but to be really successful on your Runway of Life you need to be passionate for 30 years. Live your passion and don't be concerned that some people will mistake passion for luck. There's no way you can be "just lucky" for 30 years.

In my own life, I've received every single professional speaking award — about 20 of them — you can receive in Canada. Now, maybe I lucked out with the first two, the others I had to work damn hard for, studying, reading and practicing. I presented hundreds of free speeches to hone my craft, in addition to working with voice coaches and spending considerable hours developing my materials, all with great passion and enthusiasm. That's why I know in my heart that nobody could ever say I was "just lucky." Luck is really the result of hard work and a commitment — with passion — to your dreams and visions.

Obviously, it is difficult to be passionate about every single thing you do. That's why it is essential that you are truly passionate about your primary purpose. For instance, I am absolutely passionate about speaking, but I don't like flying. The paradox is that in order to do what I am passionate about, I also have to do the very thing that I don't like.

I have decided that I am willing to put aside my fear in

order to obtain my goal. In fact, just as this book is going into production, I will be leaving on a two-week trip to Australia. That's a 29-hour trip. I told my wife Kay, who will be travelling to Australia with me, "I'd pay $20,000 not to go on that flight."

So why am I going? Basically, because it is an opportunity that I'm not willing to miss out on. It is also a trip that I was planning to take a couple of years ago. At that time, a fellow by the name of Mike Doughty, who owns and operates a business development company called The Knowledge Gym in Auckland, New Zealand, had contacted me and booked a few speaking engagements for me throughout Australia. Unfortunately, I had a stroke and had to cancel the trip.

When the Variety Club International decided to have their 2004 convention in Sydney, Australia, I called Mike up again and told him I was going to be available. He got back to me and said, "We've got three dates booked for you in Christchurch, Wellington and Auckland the week before your convention." This is shaping up to be the perfect business trip and in spite of the prospect of the long flight, I'm starting to get excited.

Over 1,500 years ago, Papyrus said, "If you can't get enthusiastic about your work, it's time to get alarmed, something is wrong! Compete with yourself, set your teeth and dive into the job of breaking your own record. No one keeps up his enthusiasm automatically. Enthusiasm must be nourished with new actions, new aspirations, new efforts and new vision. It is one's own fault if enthusiasm is gone, he has failed to feed it. If you want to turn your hours into minutes, renew your enthusiasm."

PASSION Do's and Don'ts

Five things you should definitely do and just a few don'ts

Let's start with the don'ts. First of all, you absolutely don't need to quit your current job or career to rush off and find your passion. In fact, such a drastic move is more likely to bring you unnecessary stress than it is to result in your finding your true passion.

Secondly, for heaven's sake, don't let anyone tell you that you are too old, too entrenched in your career or expecting too much because you want to be passionate about the life you are living.

Finally, don't worry about whether or not your passion is practical in terms of "career potential." The truth is that for most of us, once we find something that we are truly passionate about, we will find a way to make it a part of our life whether or not that includes making it our "work."

Now, if you're ready, here are some suggestions for finding, or rediscovering, your own passion.

Start off simple

This is the best approach with anything in life. In this case, start by simply doing something for yourself. Try joining a group that participates in an activity that interests you, or sign up to learn something new, perhaps by taking an art course or history class at the local community college. This is a great way to meet others who are passionate about the things that interest you.

If you're not sure what you're looking for, check out college and university brochures and continuing education flyers or browse through a listing of community organizations to see what catches your interest.

It's the journey, not the destination!

Many people lose their passion in pursuit of goals because they forget to take some time to enjoy the journey. It's like getting in your car and driving non-stop from Seattle to New York. Sure, it's an accomplishment to arrive at your destination, but think of all the great people, places and experiences you missed along the way by rushing to get there.

One way to make sure you enjoy the milestones along the way is to take time out each day to reflect on and share — with family, friends or co-workers — both the successes and the memorable moments you had that day, however small they may be. This is also a great way to acknowledge the contribution of others and to recharge everyone's passion for a shared goal or project.

Oh, the people you'll meet

Take time to connect with the people you meet as you travel along your Runway of Life. As any writer will tell you, everybody has a story, you just have to take the time to find out what it is. The payoff here is that the best ideas you will ever have are going to result from talking — and listening — to other people.

I got the idea to write this book from my friend Joe, not because I called him up and asked him to give me a great concept for a book, but because Joe and I regularly get together to have lunch and talk about life.

Change your point of view

You know the old saw, "If you always do what you have always done, you will always get what you have always gotten"? Well, I am here to tell you that it is still true. That's why it is important to make change a regular part of your life, even in small ways.

Why not try some of these suggestions: drive to work via a different route, buy your groceries at a store you've never been to, talk to strangers, go to the local visitors bureau and take a guided tour of your own city and see things from a different perspective. Change is a great catalyst. Not only does it break up the routine and make everyday life more interesting, it also opens us up to new opportunities, new experiences, new ideas and new people.

New mountains to climb

As your passion moves you onward and upward, keep in mind that it is not uncommon to lose some of your momentum as you check goals off of your list. Losing your momentum isn't the same as losing your passion; more often, it is the result of having reached a plateau.

So, what do you do? The same thing that any experienced mountain climber would do. Take a bit of time to catch your breath, admire the view and reflect on what worked and what didn't on your way up.

After that, you need to refocus your efforts on the peaks ahead and make sure that the goals you have set are challenging enough to keep feeding your passion. If they are not, set your sights on new mountains. Personally, I've never met a climber who was ready to stop after just one mountain.

CHAPTER 14

Enthusiasm is Contagious, Spread it Around

A lot of you may not know this, but a few years ago I suffered a pretty serious stroke. For anyone who makes their living as a public speaker — something I have been doing for more than 35 years — a stroke can be a career-ending experience. This is because it can often seriously damage the centres in the brain that control both the ability to speak and to comprehend language.

Thankfully, after many months of rehabilitation, I recovered fully. In fact, I would say that since my stroke, I am better than ever before. Perhaps because I came out of the situation with a renewed appreciation for the fragility of life and a determination to make the most of every moment left on my runway.

Often, in the question and answer period following one of my speeches, someone will ask me, "Why is it that you are so energetic?" I suspect, in part it comes from a belief that you are as happy as you make up your mind to be. Another part comes from the fact that as an only child of parents who were loving and encouraging, I always knew that my mom and dad truly believed in me. Although they were not wealthy during my early years living in England, they worked hard and saved money to be able to send me to private school. I always wanted them to be proud of me and I wanted to be successful and have my life amount to something to show them just how much I appreciated all they had sacrificed for me. But perhaps the most important source of energy, the thing that drives me forward is an enthusiasm for the work that I do, for the people I share my life with and for the opportunities to learn and grow that are opened up for me every time I give my time and energy to others.

In my experience, enthusiasm is one of the most combustible elements known to man. All it takes is a little spark to ignite and you have a boundless source of energy.

The word enthusiasm comes from the Greek root "entheos" and means "God within." It refers to the fire that burns within those who have a passion for a cause, their work or life in general.

Enthusiastic people are imaginative, inspirational and just plain enjoyable to be around. I've found that while it's almost impossible to succeed without enthusiasm, regardless of how clever or talented you might be, it's also quite difficult, with enough enthusiasm, to fail. Life really is a self-fulfilling prophecy. If you expect to set the world on fire, you're likely to be successful. Likewise, if you think you're going to fall flat on your face, you probably will.

Once it is set in motion, enthusiasm can be a perpetual motion machine propelling us toward success. All we have to do is wind it up and it creates its own energy. Therefore, the more enthusiastic we are, the more enthusiastic we'll know ourselves to be. Enthusiasm is also highly contagious, it spreads quickly to others. When we show enthusiasm, the energy pours out of us like a flood, it spills over and rushes off in every direction, flowing freely and wetting everything in its path.

So, how do you develop enthusiasm in your own life? It begins with gratitude and awareness. Look around at all that you have in your life. Your family and the love they give you; your home and the comfort it provides; your career and the security it offers; your friends and the support they contribute.

Charles Kingsley once said, "We act as though comfort and luxury were the chief requirements of life, when all that we need to make us happy is something to be enthusiastic about." If you are having trouble getting enthusiastic about your life, start keeping a journal. At the end of each day, sit down with your journal and write down at least five things that you are grateful for. With all of the little things that we take for granted every day, this is a good way to remind ourselves of the abundance we actually have. It is also a good time to work on developing and writing down goals if you are not already doing this.

I know that some of you are probably thinking, "How can I be enthusiastic when I don't like my job?" Do you remember how I said that enthusiasm is contagious? Well, the reverse is also true. No one wants to work with someone who is negative, pessimistic, or worse yet, indifferent. If you are feeling frustrated and depressed, chances are your attitude is affecting the people around you.

Maybe it's time to turn on your mental ignition; get excited, and let your enthusiasm be a spark for others. One of the most powerful aspects of enthusiasm is that it breaks down both obstacles and objections. When we value and appreciate what we have in our life, we have more energy to overcome obstacles and more determination to defeat objections.

When you are enthusiastic at work, you inspire others and gain their cooperation. That said, don't waste your time and energy hanging out with negative people; instead, develop a circle of enthusiastic and optimistic friends. If you need to meet some new people to do this, consider joining a service club or doing some volunteer work. People who offer their time freely to others are usually enthusiastic.

One of the special abilities of enthusiastic people is the ability to see value in situations that would normally discourage other people. This is because enthusiasm comes from a deep place inside of us, not from the situation we find ourselves in.

Martha Washington has been quoted as saying, "The

greatest part of our happiness or misery depends on our dispositions, and not our circumstances." It is true that the difference between success and failure, as often as not, depends on what we choose to do when we face a daunting task and feel like quitting. Successful lives require effort. Success requires a greater investment and a willingness to go the extra mile. While it may not be noticeable immediately, putting your whole heart into what you do pays off in the long run. Giving half of our best will yield just half of the results.

Of course, not only will enthusiasm make you more productive, it can also make light of difficult tasks. As we all know, every worthy project has some aspects to it that are dull and routine but nevertheless important to the accomplishment of our goal. Keeping the end result in mind will build enthusiasm for the difficult tasks you encounter along the way and give you energy to succeed.

In addition to being contagious, enthusiasm also has a magnetic quality about it. If you watch someone who enjoys life and approaches every situation with enthusiasm, you cannot help but notice how that energy affects the people around them. It is the special energy that makes someone like the Dalai Lama so fascinating to people of all faiths; it is also the special energy that makes one community soccer program the envy of all the surrounding communities or one home on a street the meeting place for all the children in the neighbourhood.

People are magnetically drawn to positive energy. It is

also true that when people sense your enthusiasm, they will often go out of their way to help you succeed. It is a good reason to keep your enthusiasm alive, and you will attract many people who are willing to help you accomplish your goals.

In my own life, enthusiasm has been the key to making my dream of motivating and inspiring others come true. When I leave the stage after speaking to an audience, people aren't lining up to tell me how much they admire my intellect or my business sense. What they are eager to share is how one of my stories touched them or got them excited about making a change in their own life. They tell me that they are inspired by my enthusiasm for life and the sincerity of my message.

Think of all the successful people you admire. Whether they are athletes, entertainers, business leaders, mentors or parents — the best people, those who shine, have one thing in common, an enthusiasm for what they are doing. Denis Waitley said, "Get excited and enthusiastic about your own dream. This excitement is like a forest fire — you can smell it, taste it and see it from a mile away."

Isn't it time you set the world on fire? Dare to be enthusiastic!

Five Ways to Fire Up Your Enthusiasm

First of all, talk the talk. Speak in a cheerful voice and start focusing and talking more about what is going right in every situation. Part of this is changing the words you choose to describe situations. For example, instead of saying that someone is "stubborn," consider that they are "passionate" in their beliefs. Likewise, instead of saying "I'm overworked," you could say "I'm ambitious." When you feel "exhausted," why not say that you are "recharging." Not only will you feel better emotionally when you use a positive tone, others too will respond more readily to the positive energy you are giving off.

Now, walk the walk. Change your body language. Straighten your spine and let the energy flow through your entire body. When you walk, do it with purpose; take bigger steps and walk faster. When you speak to others, look them in the eye and give them your full attention. Your body language is just as important as your words in expressing your interest and enthusiasm.

Next, change your perspective; focus on solutions rather than problems. Use your energy to visualize what you want, not to worry about what you don't want. Focus on how you can succeed, not on how you might fail. Eliminate the word "but" from your vocabulary. "But" is simply a big eraser that rubs out everything that came before it. Recognize and acknowledge the effort that others put into a project, not just the end result.

Go out of your way to avoid energy leeches. "It's hard to stop people from stepping on you if you keep lying down under their feet," says Michael Mercer, business psychologist and co-author of the book *Spontaneous Optimism*. According to Mercer, if you feel someone is trying to suck the enthusiasm out of you, realize that you're letting them do it. Pull the plug on unhealthy relationships by choosing not to associate yourself with pessimists and negative people.

Finally, be a role model for everyone around you. Think of yourself as a mirror, reflecting the kind of energy and attitude you would like others to display. When the people around you look into the mirror, what do you want them to see? Remember, enthusiasm is contagious. Spread it around and it will quickly multiply and flow back to you.

CHAPTER 15

Attitude

No one has the same beliefs at 60 years of age as they had at 20 and yet one of the oldest, simplest and most direct paths to the success we seek on our runway of life is that of an optimist, to face every day with a positive attitude.

I didn't write the line, "Your attitude determines your altitude," which my mentor Mel Cooper once quoted to me. I wish I had. If I had a dollar for every time I've quoted it myself, or read it in a book, seen it in a training video, or heard it on a CD or tape recording, I'd be a very rich man indeed.

Sir Winston Churchill said, "I am an optimist. It doesn't seem too much use being anything else."

Abraham Lincoln observed, "The pessimist sees the difficulty in every opportunity, the optimist sees the opportunity in every difficulty."

Dr. Thomas J. Stanley's marvellous book *The Millionaire Mind* researched 1,000 millionaires and discovered that a whopping 62 per cent claimed they were millionaires because of their ability to get along with other people.

W. Clement Stone once said, "I can't guarantee you will be successful with a positive attitude, but I can guarantee you won't be without one."

It seems so obvious to me that a more successful life, both personal and corporate, can only really be lived when we have powerful positive attitudes. No, I am not talking about a Pollyanna or Mary Poppins approach to life but a deep feeling of "I'm happy to be alive — I am living a life of significance, people like hanging around me, my attitude is infectious and life is for the taking."

Every great leader possesses this positive attitude even though they know that "Life is tough — get used to it. Life isn't fair — get over it."

Most of the decisions we make are based on our present state of mind and the attitude we decide to have every day. You have heard the statistic that if we repeat something for 21 days, it becomes a habit in our life.

Abraham Lincoln said, "We are about as happy as we make up our minds to be." Paraphrased: We have about as positive an attitude as we make up our minds to have. It all really comes down to choice and it's those choices we make that determine our success in life, and the first choice of the day, the choice to approach whatever the day may hold with a positive attitude, is critical.

Psychiatrists say the first encounter of the day affects the next 13! Think about those people you meet and greet in the first 90 minutes of the day — your spouse, your children, the neighbours, the guy behind the counter at Starbucks Coffee, the person filling your tank at the gas station, your receptionist, your assistant, your staff, the person on the other end of the line when you make your first phone call of the day. We affect or infect everybody with our attitude.

Whether we like it or not, our attitude is everything. And as I've mentioned in a previous chapter, if you have a positive attitude and live to 60, you will have no chronic illness, so there is even a health benefit to having a positive attitude. Think about what kind of people you want to hang around with, and then take a look in the mirror. You don't want to be the kind of person who brightens a room by leaving it, do you?

So first thing tomorrow morning when the opportunity clock goes off (that's what Zig Ziglar calls it), jump out of bed, strip off naked, stand in front of the mirror, look at yourself and say, "I am unstoppable" and then jump. Even the image of performing this will bring a smile to your face because some things will jiggle around that you haven't seen before — and that will definitely bring a smile to your face.

Now you're ready for the day. So get out there, and remember, when you meet the first person of the day and they ask you how you are this morning, you're going to proudly say, "I'm fantastic, thanks for asking," regardless of how you feel (because in reality they don't care; they aren't really listening). But that doesn't matter one bit, because when you say, "I'm fantastic," you do two things. First of all, you surprise them, and secondly, you begin to reinforce for yourself what a smashing day it will be when you purpose it so.

I was recently speaking at the Mirage Hotel in Las Vegas for Jaguar Canada and had to take an early flight from Las Vegas to San Francisco. Upon leaving the hotel at 5:30 a.m., dressed in a smart business suit, I bounded up to the checkout counter, manned by a young fellow in his twenties, to pay the bill.

Other than a couple of diehards playing blackjack and a few people on the slot machines, no one else was around. As I approached the counter, the young man, who was just finishing his shift, asked rather grumpily, "How are you this morning?" "Just fantastic, thank you," I replied. To this he said, again in a rather sombre voice, "And what makes you so fantastic this morning?"

I thought quickly and responded, "You know, young man, 3,200 60-year-old men didn't wake up this morning. They're dead." He looked at me with a startled expression on his face and then suddenly he brightened a little and said, "I'm starting to feel better already."

Now I have no idea if that statistic is true or not; I just made it up on the spot because I had a big day ahead of me and I didn't want any negativity from him to slip into my spirit. I paid my bill, bounced out of the hotel feeling great and hopefully affected the next 13 people with my positive attitude — the bellman, the cab driver, the ticket agent, the security guard, the coffee shop attendant, the airline check-in clerk, the air hostess, my seat mate and ultimately my next audience in San Francisco.

Pastor Chuck Swindoll has made famous his affirmation on attitudes. "The longer I live, the more I realize the impact of attitude on life. Attitude to me is more important than facts, it is more important than the past, than education, than money, than circumstances, than failures, than successes, than what other people think or say or do. It is more important than appearance, giftedness or skill. It will make or break a company, a church, a home. The remarkable thing is we have a choice every day regarding the attitude we will embrace for that day. We cannot change our past; we cannot change the fact that people will act in a certain way. We cannot change the inevitable. The only thing we can do is play on the one string we have, and that is our attitude. I am convinced that life is 10 per cent what happens to me and 90 per cent how I react to it. And so it is with you. We are all in charge of our attitudes!"

Your attitude is a little thing that makes a big difference. The dictionary defines attitude as "one's feelings or mood toward things and people." Well, if our life is dealing with people virtually every day, then we must believe noted University of Pennsylvania psychologist Martin Seligman who says, "Individuals who are optimistic and have a positive attitude are more successful than similarly talented pessimists."

CHAPTER 16

Tenacity

When I asked my good friend and mentor, Joe Segal, what one characteristic is a sure-fire indicator that someone will turn out to be a successful person, he was quick to answer.

"Tenacity!" he exclaimed. "The ability to pick yourself up, regroup and keep going when you encounter obstacles on your runway." According to Joe, failure is a fact of life, and a great learning opportunity.

"The secret to success, the thing that many people never figure out," Joe told me, "is that we all fail many times before we succeed. I've always believed that experience is the best teacher. I say, show me a person who is a failure and I will show you someone who gave up while success still lay before them. Then show me a person who is a success and I will show you someone with many failures behind him. Failure is an event, not a person."

Joe concluded that while having a special talent or ability is no doubt a great advantage, unless it is developed and applied, it is no guarantee of success. Likewise, acquiring specialized knowledge or training can also contribute to your success; however, it is only valuable to the extent that you are prepared to apply it.

In the end, some of the most successful people in the world, including Joe himself — those who have excelled beyond what most of us could even imagine — are not the most talented or even the most educated. They are the individuals who are able to stand committed to one goal or purpose come hell or high water.

Speaking of tenacious individuals, I am a huge admirer of Sir Winston Churchill. While on a recent speaking trip to New York for Quebecor World — a $16-billion company headquartered in Montreal — I ended up in one of my favourite haunts, a New York bookstore where I found a leather-bound first edition of *Never Give In* signed by Winston S. Churchill, Sir Winston's grandson. The book was number 1,222 of 1,225 — almost the last copy.

This precious book has the best of Winston Churchill's speeches — he was nicknamed The Bulldog for his determination, commitment and tenacity — including his immortal speech delivered on June 18, 1940, before a packed House of Commons in which Churchill wanted to quell suggestions that Britain might soon succumb to the German onslaught as France had.

Many consider this speech one of his finest and it certainly demonstrated Churchill's unwavering commitment to defending England come hell or high water. On the day before that speech Churchill had said, "The news from France is very bad. The gallant French people have fallen into the terrible misfortune." However, the Germans had underestimated the tenacity of the newly elected prime minister. The very next day he delivered this remarkable speech:

"I expect the Battle of Britain is about to begin. Upon this battle depends the survival of Christian civilization. Upon it depends our own British life and the long continuity of our institution and our empire. The whole fury and might of the enemy must very soon be turned on us. Hitler knows that he will have to break us in this island, or lose the war. If we can stand up to him, all Europe may be freed and the life of the world may move forward into broad and sunlit uplands. But if we fail, then the whole world, including the United States and all that we have known and cared for, will sink into the abyss of a new dark age made more sinister and perhaps more prolonged by the lights of perverted science. Let us therefore brace ourselves to our duty and so bear ourselves that if the British Empire and Commonwealth lasts for a thousand years, men will still say, 'This is their finest hour.'"

It was a long and bloody battle. I was born just outside London in 1942, about halfway through the war. Thank goodness Churchill's commitment, which inspired all of the Allies, was unwavering. He showed tenacity at its zenith.

I recall another inspiring speech delivered by Churchill, this time to a group of young people. It was October 29,

1941, and Churchill had been invited to deliver the convocation address at the institution where he had received his education, Harrow School. You can imagine the excitement and tension in the air as this great statesman entered the school's Great Hall to deliver the convocation address. The anticipation of the crowd was palpable as Churchill was introduced. At which point he stepped up to the podium in his three-piece suit, his bowtie and his spectacles and in his booming voice told the assembled students, "Never give in. Never give in. Never, never, never, never; in nothing great or small, large or petty; never give in, except to convictions of honour and good sense."

Football coach George Allen often said, "People of mediocre ability sometimes achieve outstanding success because they don't know when to quit. Most men succeed because they are determined to." He also said, "Each of us has been put on this earth with the ability to do something well. We cheat ourselves and the world if we don't use that ability as best we can."

Allen himself lived for coaching. During 12 years in the National Football League he never had a losing season and although he never won a Super Bowl ring, of all the coaches in the Pro Football Hall of Fame, only Vince Lombardi had a higher career winning percentage. But Allen's success wasn't because he had a flashy style or exciting plays. In fact, it was just the opposite. Allen was often criticized for his unexciting offence and for trading away his draft choices in favour of seasoned veteran players, year after year.

So how did he do it? A lot of football people believed the reason Allen was able to take his team to the playoffs again and again was because he'd managed to convince his players that they were better than they ever thought they'd be. Allen was absolutely committed to discipline, conditioning and an extraordinary attention to detail. "Winning," he explained, "is the science of being totally prepared."

I want you to take a moment right now and ask yourself this question, "What great thing would I attempt to do if I knew I could not fail?" Because the truth is, you really can't fail. You can only fail to try.

In the bible, Chapter 12, Verse 1 of Hebrews says, "Let us run with perseverance the race marked out for us." Although we may sometimes be surprised by how the road winds and turns along the way, we shouldn't take it to mean we have gone off course.

Do you think that Nelson Mandela knew when he first chose to raise his voice against apartheid in South Africa that he would spend more than 27 years of his life in a prison cell? Amazingly, when he was released from prison, Mandela was neither bitter nor discouraged. With his optimism, hope and a willingness to forgive his captors and forge a new start, Nelson Mandela set an example for all of his countrymen. He went on to become the first post-apartheid president of South Africa, to begin the process of reconciliation and healing between blacks and whites, and realize his dream of a democratic South Africa. Who is to say what the world would look like today if Mandela had not had the tenacity to persevere?

Albert Einstein is quoted as saying, "It's not that I'm so smart, it's just that I stay with problems longer." Even if Einstein was being hopelessly modest in this statement, his line of reasoning is compelling. The world would never have benefited from his theories and equations if he had not pursued them far beyond the point where even the most dedicated theoretician would likely have given up (that's why there's only ever been one Einstein). Of his approach to problems, Einstein said, "I think and think for months and years. Ninety-nine times, the conclusion is false. The hundredth time I am right." Imagine the determination it must take to be wrong 99 per cent of the time and still keep your mind focused on getting to that one time when you finally get it right.

Marabel Morgan is quoted as saying, "Persistence is the twin sister of excellence. One is a matter of quality; the other, a matter of time."

We have many tenacious individuals to thank for the conveniences of our modern world. Thomas Edison, inventor of the incandescent light bulb among many other things, was famous for the fact that it took him thousands of attempts before he was successful (he was definitely a fellow determined to look on the bright side when things didn't go according to plan).

"Results! . . . I have gotten a lot of results," said Edison. "I know several thousand things that don't work." This tenacity earned him the backing of financiers J.P Morgan and the Vanderbilts, who established the Edison Light Company and advanced Edison $30,000 for research and development. It also cemented Edison's reputation as the world's greatest inventor of his age and guaranteed him a place in the history books.

"The harder you work, the harder it is to surrender," said Vince Lombardi.

Earl Nightingale said, "Difficult things take a long time, impossible things a little longer. Don't let the fear of the time it will take to accomplish something stand in the way of your doing it. The time will pass anyway; we might just as well put that passing time to the best possible use."

There was a point in my own life where my dissatisfaction with having "just a job" and answering to someone else's desires overcame any fear or uncertainty I had about becoming an entrepreneur. At once, I realized that I needed to be in control of my own destiny, yet the only way to make it happen was for me to bite the bullet and take a chance. That's exactly what I did.

If you remember back to the first chapter of this book, the chapter about Joe, I told you the story about how I first met him when I was selling advertising for the radio station CJOR and he had his office in the back of one of his Fields department stores. Now you may have wondered when you read that story, why I kept going back to see Joe again and again despite the fact that he kept telling me he wasn't going to buy any advertising from me. The truth is I admired the man — he started out in business with very little money, but a whole lot of determination and ambition — and I wanted to be like him. I wanted to be successful and I figured the best way to learn how to do that was by modelling myself after people like Joe who were living the kind of life I wanted for myself.

I think the other reason I returned was because Joe always encouraged me, he told me to dream big and then go after my dream with everything I had in me. Although he never bought any advertising from me, Joe told me that he admired my persistence. He seemed to think that that persistence could more than make up for whatever I lacked in experience or financial resources. And so when the opportunity to buy a little publication called *TV WEEK* and become a magazine publisher popped up, I knew it was now or never, and I jumped with both feet.

I soon found out that not everyone was as supportive as Joe. In fact, I was rather surprised at how many people — friends and associates — thought I had taken leave of my senses. "What do you know about publishing?" they asked me. "What, are you crazy, there's no money in magazines," they said. That skepticism didn't go away for a long time — at our five, 10 and even 15-year anniversaries, I still encountered people who expected the bottom to fall out at any moment — but I didn't let that stop me; I had a dream. I determined that my little company, Canada Wide Magazines & Communications Ltd., would add one new magazine a year to its publication list.

In April 2006, Canada Wide will celebrate 30 years in business, and guess what? We currently publish 31 different magazine titles, so technically we're actually ahead of the game at this point. On top of that, as a $25-million company, we are the largest independent publisher in Western Canada with a head office in Burnaby, B.C., and sales offices in both Calgary and Toronto. It has been, at once, more exciting, more challenging and more rewarding than I ever imagined.

Edward B. Butler said, "One man has enthusiasm for 30 minutes, another for 30 days, but it is the man who has it for 30 years who makes a success of his life."

Now, at the same time that I was establishing my publishing company, I also became involved with a number of community organizations including the Variety Club, where I had the opportunity to do some public speaking, something I soon realized I have a true passion for. However, when I shared my idea that I would like to become a professional speaker, I didn't get the encouragement I had hoped for. "You'll never earn a living, there's so much competition," several people told me, while others concluded, "It's fine to do a speech now and then to raise the profile of your company, just don't let it get in the way of your business. You can't run a publishing company and be a professional speaker."

As I've said elsewhere, although people are quick to tell you what you *can't* do, they will rarely tell you what you *can* do. As I set out on the road to become a professional speaker,

I had to trust in my conviction that I had a valuable contribution to make as a motivational speaker. Fortunately, as I began to meet other speakers and join professional organizations I did receive encouragement towards my goal.

Earl Nightingale told me, "If you learn to be an accomplished speaker, the doors that will open to you will take you beyond your wildest dreams." Little did I know just how right he was, although at the time I thought, "Sure, easy for you to say, you're Earl Nightingale, a world-famous speaker and commentator."

So, did it happen overnight? No, it took me many years to learn my craft. Was it an easy undertaking? Certainly not! It took me an enormous amount of work. First I had to study and learn the fundamentals of public speaking. I did this by attending every workshop that the National Speakers Association and the Canadian Association of Public Speakers conduct. I attended presentations by literally hundreds of great speakers because I wanted to learn from the very best. I read every book I could get my hands on that was involved with public speaking. I practiced every day on my timing, delivery and content. I also developed my voice and spent countless hours honing my craft until it looked easy.

Next, I had to get some experience under my belt. To do this, I delivered hundreds of free speeches to organizations of all sizes and types to develop my reputation as a speaker. I've heard it said that it takes seven or eight years to master a skill — it's definitely not for the faint of heart or those with a short attention span — I guess that's why it's called mastery.

Was it worth all the time and effort? Absolutely! I'm proud to say that I have received many distinguished awards for professional speaking, including Toastmasters International's Golden Gavel Award, the Oscar of public speaking. In addition, Toastmasters International named me one of the Top Five Speakers in North America. I have also received The National Speakers Association designation of Certified Speaking Professional (C.S.P.) and the coveted Council of Peers Award of Excellence (C.P.A.E.). Not bad for a little kid born in England (although I wasn't born on the wrong side of the tracks, I wasn't born with a silver spoon in my mouth either). In addition, I have been inducted into the Speakers Hall of Fame, the highest award for speaking excellence and professionalism bestowed by the National Speakers Association in the United States and the Canadian Speakers Hall of Fame (HOF).

More than the awards and recognitions, the best part for me as a speaker is the fact that I can interact on such a personal level with so many people. I get more personal satisfaction from public speaking than from almost anything else in my professional life. It's the biggest thrill to know that I can stand up in front of an audience and in the course of an hour spent sharing my stories and anecdotes, I can make them laugh, bring them to tears and inspire them enough that when they leave the room they are ready to take on the world on their own terms.

In closing this chapter, I would like to leave you with this poem written by Hazrat Inayat Khan, founder of the Sufi Order in the West, in the hopes that it will inspire you to see the opportunity in every obstacle you encounter along your runway.

I asked for strength, and God gave me difficulties
to make me strong.
I asked for wisdom, and God gave me problems
to learn to solve.
I asked for prosperity, and God gave me a brain
and brawn to work.
I asked for courage, and God gave me dangers to overcome.
I asked for love, and God gave me people to help.
I asked for favours, and God gave me opportunities.
I received nothing I wanted.
I received everything I needed.

CHAPTER 17

Write Your Own Obituary

Stephen Covey, author of the best-selling groundbreaking book *Seven Habits of Highly Effective People,* sometimes tells his seminar audiences to "find a quiet place and go and write your own obituary" — a rather sombre task. Covey is not trying to be morbid; rather, he explains that it is a useful way of deciding what we wish to accomplish and what really matters to us in life.

On this runway of life, it is a fact that where we put our time and effort is where we will gain the greatest rewards. With this in mind, we need to take a look at our goals and dreams from the other end. Are they going to get us where we want to go?

If we truly want to make the most of our runway, each of us must make certain that we have our priorities in place. Writing our own obituary is an excellent way to test our priorities. "What is it we would like to be said about us when we are gone?"

I wonder how many of us have heard a speaker, pastor, friend or family member tell us how important it is to live our life backwards, or put another way, live our life with the end in mind. The runway of life is short, so we might begin thinking about it now. We are not going to be there when family and friends pay their last respects.

Lord Baden Powell, the founder of the Boy Scouts movement, is said to have lived out the precept that every minute was "60 seconds" worth of distance run. Within a century of its founding, there were Boy Scout troops in 110 nations. What a legacy!

I first heard the following quote from professional speaker Willy Jolly at a national speakers' convention in Orlando, then I read it in Herman Cain's book, *CEO of Self,* and he attributed it to Dr. Benjamin E. Mays of Morehouse College in Atlanta:

God's Minute

I've only just a minute
Only 60 seconds in it
Forced upon me, can't refuse it
Didn't seek it, didn't choose it
But it's up to me to use it
Give an account if I abuse it
Just a tiny little minute
But eternity is in it.

Obviously, it's how we spend those minutes and how wisely we use our time on our runway that will determine our character, and eventually how we develop our character will really determine our own legacy and what people say about us in the end.

Sir Winston Churchill once said, "What is the use of living, if it be not to strive for noble causes and to make this muddled world a better place to live after we are gone."

Clement Attlee said that Churchill was the greatest Englishman of our time, but I think he was the greatest citizen of the world of our time.

Churchill died at the age of 91 in his home in London on January 24, 1965. He had apparently written out the arrangements for his funeral saying he wanted "lots of bands." His body lay in state in Westminster Hall for three days and more than 300,000 people filed past his coffin night and day to pay their last respects. Six thousand people attended his funeral including the Queen of England, five other sovereigns and 15 presidents and prime ministers.

Following the service at St. Paul's Cathedral he was returned to his birthplace at Blenheim Palace next to his parents and his brother Jack. His runway had finally come to its end. Author Robin Neillands calls Churchill the Statesman of the Century.

The founder of the Salvation Army, William Booth, died in 1912 at the age of 83 and it was as if a head of state had passed away. Some 65,000 people came to view his body in state. Monarchs sent wreaths. Behind the funeral cortege, 5,000 members of the famed and highly respected Salvation

Army marched six abreast.

Another legacy — another runway come to an end. Powell, Churchill and Booth all had character and lived their purpose and passion.

In James L. Garlow's book, *21 Irrefutable Laws of Leadership Tested by Time*, the author says, "Character is best learned early, but if you don't learn it early, at least learn it late. Just make sure you learn it."

Closer to home, my wife Kay and I were on an assignment at Disney World in Florida and played a game of golf at one of the Disney golf courses. We were teamed up with a fellow named Jack Haley and his wife. They both looked a little old for us and we thought that this game was to be a cinch — no competition at all. How wrong we were!

Jack was two under par by the ninth hole — the turn, as they call it. He walked very slowly to the men's washroom, almost purposefully, and then Kay and I went into action with his wife. "Tell us all about Jack! Who is he? How old is he? How does he play so well?" we asked her.

She told us that Jack was a retired PGA pro and that they came to Orlando from time to time.

"Why does he walk so slowly?" I asked. She told me he had had an operation on his heart and it didn't take.

"He is on constant medication, but no more operations, they are too dangerous," she said. "You see, Peter, he is going to die."

I asked, "When?"

She said, "It could happen at any minute."

Just then, Jack returned to our foursome and we continued the back nine. I asked him about the pending end to his runway of life and how he handled it moment by moment.

Jack simply told me, "Play to your strengths. Have courage and develop your character in life so that people speak well of you when you are gone."

Jack's advice brings us back to Steven Covey's exercise, "What would you like people to say about you when you are gone?" While you think about that, I would like to share with you excerpts from eulogies I had the great honour to present for two of Vancouver's greatest.

The first eulogy was for Tong Louie, who lived his life wanting to be known as an ordinary, hard-working fellow. Although hard work was the very essence of the man, during his lifetime, Tong Louie demonstrated in a multitude of ways that he was, in fact, quite extraordinary.

According to his biographer, E.G. Perrault, "Tong Louie was, by the time he died, one of the leading industrialists in Western Canada, one of its most active philanthropists, and a patriarch of one of its pioneering social groups, but with the modesty that was his defining characteristic, he claimed little public attention for any of this."

As the second of 11 children born to Chinese immigrant parents, Tong Louie learned early in life the values that would lead to his success.

In 1934, Tong's father, Hok Yat Louie (the H.Y. in H.Y.

Louie Co. Ltd.), wrote three letters to his sons while he was in Hong Kong and his sons were in Vancouver. His letters were simple truths that at the time were intended as guiding rules for the new Louie business.

In his first letter he wrote:

"When pursuing prosperity, you must follow the laws of heaven. Don't be afraid to be kind and charitable . . . ill deeds should be avoided."

In his second letter he told his sons to preserve their own reputations:

"Be earnest, fair and loyal in your dealings with customers."

And in his third letter he instructed his sons on one precious lesson:

"Develop your own character as well as your working skills."

For more than half a century, Hok Yat's words have been a constant in the Louie family's success. Incredibly simple, completely understandable advice that came from a father who cared not just about business, but about the importance of family, of respect, of the community and of working and living together.

Tong Louie built his life, career and character on those simple truths. In recognition of the extraordinary contributions he made to the community, he was awarded the Order of B.C., the Order of Canada, the Knight of the Golden Pencil, the Astra Award and the Variety Club's Golden Heart Award.

Tong often recalled his father's words, and lived by them: "When pursuing prosperity, you must follow the rules of heaven. Don't be afraid to be kind and charitable."

"This is the story of an unsung hero most Canadians didn't know they had," wrote Perrault. Tong Louie died in April 1998 at the age of 84.

It has been said that, "Every man has a character, but few are of character." Character is founded on the living rock of principle. Over 2,500 years ago, a Chinese philosopher said, "Character is destiny." In an era when there is glory in glitz and greed, does this still apply? There is no higher praise than . . . he is a man of character.

The circumstances amid which you live determine your reputation; the truth you believe determines your character.

Reputation is what you are supposed to be; character is what you are.

Reputation is the photograph; character is the face.

Reputation comes over one from without; character grows up from within.

Reputation is what you have when you come to a new community; character is what you have when you go away.

Your reputation is made in a moment; your character is built in a lifetime.

Your reputation is learned in an hour; your character does not come to light for a year.

Reputation grows like a mushroom; character lasts like eternity.

Reputation makes you rich or makes you poor; character makes you happy or makes you miserable.

Reputation is what men say about you on your tombstone; character is what the angels say about you before the throne of God.

The second eulogy I delivered was for one of my dearest friends, Roy Lisogar. William Shakespeare once said, "All the world's a stage and all the men and women merely players. They have their exits and their entrances. And one man in his time plays many parts."

In his lifetime, my friend Roy Roger Lisogar, who died in April of 2003, played many parts. He was a Hollywood trick rider and stuntman. He owned a construction company that built 36 buildings in downtown Vancouver. He produced the Canadian ice show. He played football. He produced the Canadian Circus. He was responsible for Vancouver's first rodeo at Callister Park. He was the campaign manager for B.C. politician Grace McCarthy for 10 years.

He starred in Eastern Alberta's Senior Hockey League. He is a world record holder for a salmon caught at River's Inlet, British Columbia, in 1974. He has owned and operated 12 different hotels and 20 different restaurants. He was a street painter. He even worked for Boeing Aircraft.

THE MAN JUST COULDN'T KEEP A JOB!

But the part he loved the most, other than his family, was the part he played as a giver to the community.

Mahatma Gandhi said, "You will find yourself by losing

yourself in service to other people."

Albert Schweitzer said, "I do not know what your destiny will be, but one thing I know is the only ones among you who will be really happy are those who will have sought and found how to serve."

Socrates said, "The only way to achieve true success or happiness is to express yourself completely in service."

And a Ukrainian proverb says, "The same hammer that shatters the glass forges the steel." It was Roy's steel nerves and commitment to give back to his community, his province and his country that distinguished him and will be one of his lasting legacies.

In the 1970s he donated no less than four senior citizens homes to the Ukrainian communities in Chilliwack, Vernon and Vancouver. He was named hotelman of the year in 1994. The Vancouver Board of Trade made him a life member in 2002. He was actively involved in giving his time, talent, energy and money for the betterment of the business community.

For more than 50 years, Roy supported various communities and organizations all across Western Canada. Roy was one of those quiet behind-the-scenes contributors dedicated to the improvement and advancement of the community. It was because of his longtime support of The Variety Club of British Columbia that he was presented with Variety's highest honour in 1997 — The Golden Heart Community Achievement Award for Community Service.

Roy was well known for his love for painting. In fact, his

life was like a painting. Roy understood that our lives are drawn out for us by a master artist, but we are given the colours to print our own souls. Some days the colours we choose enrich who we are. Other days, our brushstrokes seem to leave shadows over the person we long to be. That is when we need a vision greater than our own.

If we look from afar, we can see the beauty of the light and dark hues, working together to create balance. From this perspective, we can see ways to illuminate our lives with fresh, true colours as we slowly become the masterpiece we were designed to be. Roy was a Da Vinci and Rembrandt rolled into one.

People might say that Roy Lisogar was just lucky. That's not so. He was a student of the law of giving, which says:

"The more you give of yourself without expectation of return, the more that will come back to you from the most unexpected sources." It is a law that Roy has passed along to the next generation through his daughter, Wendy Lisogar Cocchia, whom I mentor.

As I quoted Stephen Grellet in the introduction to this book, "I expect to pass through this world just once. Any good, therefore, that I can do or any kindness that I can show to any fellow creature, let me do it now. Let me not defer or neglect it, for I shall not pass this way again."

One of the namesakes of the church where the funerals for both Tong Louie and Roy Lisogar took place was the Evangelist John Wesley, who said, "Earn all you can, save all you can, but for heaven's sake give all you can." These two great men certainly did give their all.

What would you like your obituary to say? Go ahead and write it. But understand that the only real way to have the sort of obituary you want is to start living the way you'd like to be remembered.

CHAPTER 18

Of Frogs and Princes: Tales from the Networking Pond

About a year and a half ago, Darcy Rezac, managing director for The Vancouver Board of Trade, came to see me along with his wife Gayle Hallgren and associate Judy Thomson. The trio had come up with an idea for a book on networking.

As I recall, we met at the Delta Suites because I was doing a presentation at the Wosk Centre in downtown Vancouver. While we sat down for brunch, Darcy said that he, Gayle and Judy wanted to talk about the concept for their book. I was intrigued enough by the concept that I said to them, "Just go for it! You will never regret it."

Well, go for it they did. In January of 2003 they published *The Frog and Prince*: *Secrets of Positive Networking™ To Change Your Life.*

Of course, the first lives to change were those of the three authors.

They've been working non-stop ever since, trying to keep

up with the speaking engagements, presentations, seminars and training sessions that have been generated as a result of the book.

As Darcy related within the pages, the idea of using the age-old fairy tale of kissing frogs to find a prince came when he was first dating his wife Gayle. After just a few dates with Gayle, Darcy noticed that if he wished to spend time with her, he would have to book well in advance. When he questioned Gayle about the apparent fullness of her social calendar she informed him of the old saying that you have to kiss a lot of frogs before you find a prince. It looks like that philosophy really paid off for Gayle — she and Darcy have been happily married for more than 10 years.

It also paid off for the trio of authors. The book has now spawned a website, a regular spot in two daily newspapers and a large following of happy networkers.

The Frog and Prince networking philosophy is simple. To be successful in life and in business, it is vital that you and everyone else in your organization be able to network skillfully — with the literally thousands of potential customers, investors and business associates your company will meet annually.

The book lays out the steps and secrets to building and maintaining powerful, positive social networks. The steps are explained using an easy-to-remember acronym, N.E.T.W.O.R.K., with a chapter devoted to each letter. The secrets, revealed throughout the book, are the underlying philosophy and reflect the attitude of positive networkers. *The Frog and Prince* also ties in the science of the "small-world" phenomenon (the importance of weak links and random connections) with the art of networking. And, although it is a business book, the lessons learned apply to one's personal life, as well. Readers learn how to build powerful, positive social networks — for both business and life.

The Frog and Prince contains numerous networking stories based on the authors' personal experiences, techniques used by the great networkers, nuggets of practical networking information, end-of-chapter summaries for quick reference, and short, amusing frog fables to illustrate the points of each chapter. It is really a practical field guide to the art and science of networking.

"Networking is all about building positive relationships," says Darcy. "If you have something to offer someone, they will remember you built a relationship with them on a positive basis, and that's how great long-lasting relationships are created."

The Board of Trade is where Darcy really honed his craft as a networker. Managing Vancouver's chamber of commerce since 1986, Darcy oversees the organization of over 500 events each year. As a leading private-sector business association engaged in public policy, over 250,000 business cards are exchanged annually at Board events.

A science graduate of McGill University who has an MBA from The John Molson School of Business, Darcy has also worked as a senior executive in government, with General Motors and Alcan. He has represented The Board of Trade at the World Economic Forum in Davos, Switzerland, and Asia since 1989. The WEF, founded by Charles Schwab in 1971, is a six-day symposium that brings together many of the world's top business leaders, as well as the heads of international aid organizations, religious leaders and politicians.

The story of how The Vancouver Board of Trade came to be one of only 10 institutional members of the World Economic Forum in Davos is a networking classic. In 1989, Investment Canada invited the Province of British Columbia to make a presentation at the World Economic Forum as a featured region.

The premier of B.C. at the time wasn't interested; he didn't see the value in such an opportunity, but Darcy Rezac did. He gathered together a 15-person business delegation and headed off to Switzerland. There, the group made presentations and hosted a B.C. reception that was the talk of the forum — the ice that was served in the drinks at the reception had been flown in from the Stuart Glacier — and The Board was invited to join the WEF.

In the years since, the forum has been a great source of international speakers for The Board, giving Vancouver's business community access to the most influential people in the world. Now that's what I call a network.

As chair of The Board in 2002/2003, I worked closely with Darcy and experienced first-hand the power of his network. When we were in Davos together, I was truly amazed at all the people he knew by their first name, including Nobel prize winners, the CEOs of multinational corporations and high-ranking politicians.

As a motivational speaker and longtime supporter of Variety International, I have experienced the power of networking in my own life as well, including an unexpected brush with royalty that led to several unexpected opportunities. It all started in 2000 at the Variety International convention in London, England, where my wife and I attended the presentation of the humanitarian award to Sir Roger Moore (a well-known actor famous for his roles as James Bond and The Saint). Her Royal Highness, Princess Michael of Kent, was also in attendance as a special guest.

As luck would have it, following the presentation, I was introduced to the princess. During our conversation, we spoke about our shared passion for books and when I mentioned that I was also in the publishing industry, she invited me to Kensington Palace to have lunch with her and her husband on my next trip to London.

Six months later, I was in London again, this time with my middle daughter Rebecca. Arrangements had been made for my daughter and me to go to the Palace for lunch. At the lunch, Princess Michael gave me a copy of her book, *Crowned in a Far Country*, and we drank champagne. To say the least, it was a pretty fabulous event and a once-in-a-lifetime opportunity.

Also during the lunch, His Royal Highness, Prince Michael (a cousin to the Queen), happened to mention that he was planning a trip across Canada (a sort of trade mission to promote Britain's small business sector) and the discussion turned to whether it would be possible to have someone host a lunch for him in Vancouver. I told him that I knew just the right person to make it happen.

When I returned home, I contacted my friend and mentor, Joe Segal — who has a network that any royal person would be proud to call their own — and together we hosted a lunch for the prince at the Hotel Vancouver with 150 guests in attendance.

End of networking story? Not quite. If you remember, earlier in this chapter, I quoted Darcy as saying, "If you have something to offer someone, they will remember you built a relationship with them on a positive basis and that's how great long-lasting relationships are created." Based on my visit to Kensington Palace and the luncheon I arranged for the prince, I now have a point of contact with a member of the British royal family.

As it turns out, that contact may now be useful for a very worthwhile project I am involved with in Vancouver. One of the governors of The Board of Trade, Brandt Louie, is the chairman of a $15-million campaign to refurbish the Queen Elizabeth Theatre in downtown Vancouver, and I am a member of the committee that is overseeing the project. Work on the theatre is expected to be completed in 2006 and it has been decided that a gala performance should be planned for the re-opening of the theatre. Given that the theatre is named for the Queen, Brandt has asked me to invite the Prince and Princess to attend the opening-night gala.

There is no doubt that the attendance of their royal highnesses at the gala would be the icing on the cake . . . and to think that it all began with a chat about books. Of course, not every encounter we have is with royalty — there were thousands of hellos and handshakes in the years between the time I first became involved with Variety and the day I met Princess Michael — but that shouldn't stop us from treating everyone we meet as if they were royalty. After all, that's just the way we want to be treated ourselves.

Now, from *The Frog and Prince*, I would like to share with you *The Seven Secrets of Networking* to help you get out into the pond and build your own networks.

1. You have to kiss a lot of frogs to find a prince. Kissing frogs is what networking is all about. Make it a matter of habit.

2. Networking is not all about you; it's discovering what you can do for someone else. Networks are created and sustained when we discover something we can do for someone else. For some, this is a new way of viewing the world, but once realized, networking becomes easier. The pressure is off. You are in the world of positive networking.

3. Introduce yourself by name, always carry business cards and give them out. **Make it a habit.** Too many people don't follow this simple advice. Give yourself the advantage.

Be someone who does.

4. Treat everyone as equals. This makes life a whole lot easier than trying to figure out who's who. One person's frog may be another's prince or princess.

5. Give everyone the password to the network: **permission**. Give yourself — and everyone you come in contact with — permission to network. The multiplier effect of this simple secret is astonishing.

6. Learn the power of asking questions and use it. Questions are a powerful way to introduce yourself to a large or small group. Get the training to speak in public and step outside of your comfort zone; it's worth the stretch.

7. Be there and know something. You can't network effectively from behind your desk; you need to meet people. Networking is a contact sport. And there's no point being there unless you have something to contribute beyond your presence. Read, listen, seek out knowledge and share it.

The last word

I think the last word on networking has to be about following up. *The Frog and Prince* dedicates an entire chapter to this important aspect of building your network. It really is the only way you are going to turn that stack of business cards you've collected into a valuable network of people who can, in turn, connect you with their own networks.

Following up doesn't have to be time-consuming or elaborate. Remember networking secret number two? Find out what you can do for someone else. Often the "what" is information or a contact. A quick email can usually take care of business and not only will the person on the receiving end be grateful, they will also be sure to put you on their list of people who can be counted on to do what they promise.

Even if you haven't kept in touch with someone and you're feeling a bit guilty about it, don't be too quick to throw out their business card. Every year there are several opportunities for redemption — we call them holidays. Holidays such as Thanksgiving, Christmas and New Year's, or other special events, are a good time to restart a connection. You don't even need a reason; the holiday or event itself is reason enough.

Other opportunities to follow up are when you read or hear about something connected to a person or the business they are in, such as a marriage, promotion, career change or new product launch.

And one final tip before you hop into the pond. To ensure that you can follow up, when you get a business card from someone and especially when you have promised to do something, write it down so you don't forget. Memory can be a tricky thing, especially after a few glasses of wine at a reception or when you are accepting your 57th business card of the evening.

As Darcy says, "It's not the stuff you know; it's the stuff you don't know, or the stuff you have forgotten, that gets you into trouble."

Happy networking.

CHAPTER 19

Lessons on Leadership from The Board of Trade

In June 2002 I began my year-long tenure as chair of The Vancouver Board of Trade — The Board is Vancouver's chamber of commerce and the city's premier business association with more than 4,500 members. As it turned out, it was one of the most exciting, productive and eventful years of my business life. But I will confess to you right now that the decision to serve as chair is not one that I entered into lightly.

Leadership is a serious business; as such it deserves our full attention and our very best effort.

In fact, it took me a long time to decide. When Darcy Rezac, the managing director of The Board, first approached me with the idea, he told me that he had the full support of the executive behind him. Although flattered, I told him that I would have to take some time to think about it.

While it is true that we can steer ourselves in any direction we choose, none of us can accomplish very much in this life if we don't have support from others. As I've said before, I believe that no one is successful unless other people want them to be. I needed to check in with the important people in my life before embarking on this exciting challenge.

First I spoke with my family, who after some discussion of the public nature of the position, wholeheartedly supported the idea. Next, I sat down with the executive team at my company, Canada Wide Magazines & Communications, to discuss how it would affect business operations. They too said it was the opportunity of a lifetime. Finally, I considered the impact it would have on my speaking engagements and charity work, as it would require me to make The Board my first priority.

Then I asked myself one last question, "If I knew that this opportunity would never come again, could I afford to turn it down?"

My mind was made up.

Following on the heels of Carole Taylor — former media personality, councilwoman, business person extraordinaire, chair of the Canadian Broadcasting Corporation and all-around darling of Vancouver — I knew that I was going to have to fill some pretty big (red) shoes.

During her term at The Board, in her signature style, Carole had launched the much applauded and highly successful Spirit of Vancouver campaign to revitalize the city's sense of fun and community. In the back of our minds, we all wondered if SOV wouldn't just fizzle out without Carole's special energy and charisma behind it. Fortunately, the organization was built with volunteer spirit and that has been an unflagging source of enthusiasm. With the 2010 Olympic Games to prepare for, SOV is as vital and relevant as the day that Carole first launched it.

As for me, I began my year with the previously mentioned red shoes (the story of the red shoes appears later in this chapter) and a sense of anticipation. I was certainly challenged at times; no one knows everything about everything and this was a great learning opportunity.

I'm proud of the dozens of events I chaired — breakfasts, board meetings and executive meetings — including the successful Community Leadership Summit where former governor of Utah Michael Leavitt spoke about how much his state benefited from hosting the Olympic Games, and the standing room-only event with Michael Dell, chairman and CEO of Dell Computer Corporation.

I have fond memories of the people I met: politicians including Sheila Copps, Preston Manning, Stephen Harper and Sheila Fraser; and influential business leaders including Martha Piper, president of the University of British Columbia; Larry Berg, CEO of the Vancouver International Airport; and Dennis Skulsky, publisher of *The Vancouver Sun* and *The Province* newspapers. Of course, a highlight for a boy born in England was the chance to meet Queen Elizabeth on the occasion of her Golden Jubilee visit to Vancouver.

I am inspired by the places I visited, the most memorable

of which was the World Economic Forum in Davos, Switzerland. It was an opportunity to meet and learn from the world's most powerful, privileged and influential people: Bill Gates, Colin Powell, Bill and Chelsea Clinton and Phil Knight — the founder and CEO of Nike — to name a few.

Being chair was a unique opportunity to serve the business community in a great city and I loved it. As Sir Winston Churchill said, "We make a living by what we get, we make a life by what we give." My life was enriched by this experience and I would like to share with you some of the lessons I learned.

The first thing I learned was that saying yes to an opportunity to serve others opens many doors. Doors that most of us never get to peek behind. When I took on the role of chair, suddenly I had access to politicians at all levels within Canada, people were calling me for news interviews and quotes, I was hosting public forums where important issues were being discussed, I was introducing world-renowned speakers and getting the opportunity to chat with them about their ideas and experiences. Perhaps best of all, Board members from businesses of all sizes were seeking me out to share their opinions and let me know what The Board could do for them.

One of the first calls I received was from Annette Antoniak, president and CEO of the Pacific National Exhibition (PNE). After 91 years of operating in Hastings Park, the exhibition site, which includes an amusement park and wooden rollercoaster, was in jeopardy of being closed down and dismantled so it could be made into a green space for the city. A plan to move the PNE to the neighbouring city of Surrey had fallen through and the exhibition was teetering on extinction. Annette asked me if The Board of Trade could work with her in presenting her case for saving the PNE before the Vancouver City Council.

Both The Board of Trade and Spirit of Vancouver answered the call to action. The Board wrote a letter to city council in support of the PNE and then appeared with PNE representatives to present a plan before council for the city to take over the exhibition from the provincial government. Spirit of Vancouver kicked off a campaign in support of the PNE and I spoke at the launch on the PNE grounds. As a result of that campaign, the PNE received a lease extension to continue operations through 2003, and on January 1, 2004, the City of Vancouver took over management and operations of the exhibition.

The second thing I learned is that being in a public position such as this, you really have the opportunity to be a catalyst for change. To be truly effective, it is important to choose one or two specific areas to focus your energy on. I decided that it was important to be an ambassador for Vancouver and to educate people about the value of volunteerism.

I also learned that leadership presents you with a unique perspective from which you can gain insight into yourself and others. It affords you the opportunity to take a good look at yourself, to see yourself through the eyes of others and to make choices about what you stand for.

When you are the CEO of an organization with 4,500 members, people are going to let you know when they think you are doing a good job — and when you are not. It's like looking into the magnified side of a giant shaving mirror; although it reflects back your best side, it also has the ability to expose your biggest flaws. Something I learned from this is that although each of us has flaws, we also have a great deal to contribute to the world. Realizing and acknowledging our own flaws can help us to be more understanding of others.

I learned that you need to begin a dialogue from where others are, not from where you are. That means no matter how far apart your positions may be, you look for some common ground and begin working from that point.

In July 2002, Vancouver was put on the shortlist of four cities to submit a bid for the 2010 Olympic Games. The Vancouver Board of Trade was a strong supporter of the bid. However, during the bid process, concerns arose from many quarters that hosting the Olympics would divert significant resources away from our most serious and urgent community concerns, all for the benefit of the business community.

During the Community Leadership Summit later that fall, The Board thought it was important to provide a forum to discuss those concerns and look for solutions that would involve people from all corners of the community. Following the summit and a very open exchange of ideas, many more people were motivated to come forward with proposals addressing issues such as poverty, homelessness, property crime and drug addiction.

Perhaps the most important lesson I learned from this experience is that when you find yourself with an opposing view, keep in mind that people don't want you to carry on about what you **disagree on**, they want to hear what you can **agree to**. This is especially true when negotiating with grassroots organizations where people have invested a lot of personal effort and passion into a specific issue. Although you may have very different objectives, remember, you have a shared goal — to solve the problem — and that is the common ground upon which you can begin to build. In fact, this approach closely reflects one of the very first lessons that my three mentors, Mel, Joe and Ray taught me when I first started out in business. All three of these accomplished businessmen stressed to me the absolute importance of getting along with other men and women, no matter what. It is an ability that I have worked hard to develop in myself over the past 30-plus years and it is a skill that has served me well in being able to meet and greet people from all walks of life, deal with hundreds of different issues and react responsibly, comfortably and graciously in any situation.

I've learned that decisions made behind closed doors rarely work. You need to bring people along with you as you work through a problem or challenge. If you're going to have your employees and customers buy into the solution, you'd better ask them how they would solve the problem. Asking people for help also tells them that you understand the part they play in your success and it gives them an incentive to make the solution work.

I learned that humour is a powerful language, the power being that it can open us up to new ways of thinking and doing — this is a valuable tool for any leader.

When Carole Taylor became chair of The Vancouver Board of Trade in June 2001, she arrived at the Annual General Meeting (for it is there that the new chair takes on their responsibilities) wearing a beautiful red suit with matching red shoes. And when it was time for her to address the members, she delivered a moving and passionate speech on her vision as chair. At that time I was senior vice chair and chair elect for the following year. After the AGM, Board of Trade governor Bob Kadlec sought me out and said to me, "Pete, did you see that, Carole spoke flawlessly for 20 minutes without using a single page of notes. You've got big shoes to fill next year."

A year later, as it approached the time for me to take over as chair, I called Carole and (although it might be a fashion faux pas) asked her if she would do me the great favour of wearing the same red suit and shoes to my inauguration. She graciously agreed.

During my speech at the AGM, I related the story of the previous year and Bob's comment to me on Carole's performance. When I got to the point of Bob telling me I had big shoes to fill, I produced my own red shoes from under the podium — a pair of size 10 loafers painted red (see picture among the photographs in the centre of this book). Now I did this for two important reasons. The first was to cleverly pay tribute to the outstanding job Carole had performed as chair. The second was to make the audience laugh and get them on my side, while relieving some of the tension I felt in taking on the great responsibility of being chair.

In fact, laughter can help relieve tension in even the heaviest of matters. For example, during the Cuban missile crisis in the 1960s, American and Soviet negotiators found themselves deadlocked. They sat together in silence until someone suggested that each person should tell a humorous story. When it was his turn, one of the Russians offered a riddle: "What is the difference between capitalism and communism?" he asked. The answer, "In capitalism, man exploits man. In communism, it's the other way around." The tactic worked and with the mood lightened, the talks continued.

I believe that not only can you laugh at adversity, but it is necessary to do so if you are to deal with setbacks without defeat. When you do find humour in trying times, one of the first and most important changes you experience is that you see your difficulties in a new way — you suddenly have a new perspective on them. As a result of this new vantage point, you may also see new ways to deal with problems.

Finally, I learned something about the balance between the politics of business and the business of politics during my tenure. It happened about three-quarters of the way into my year as chair. Up to that point, for the most part things had gone quite smoothly. I represented The Board at a variety of functions, had the great fortune to meet a lot of great people and facilitate important economic discussions. This was the same time that the softwood lumber dispute with the U.S. was really putting a damper on cross-border trade.

Although I could sense a tension building I had no idea the part I would play as things eventually came to a climax. The situation centred around insulting comments made by several federal government officials towards the U.S. and its administration.

These comments, coming from as high up as the prime minister's office, were having a damaging effect on the relationship between the two countries as evidenced by a speech in which the U.S. ambassador urged Canada to cease and desist with the name calling or be willing to face the consequences in economic terms.

So it was, that at the March meeting of The Board's executive, Canada's deteriorating relationship with the U.S. dominated the agenda. Among Board members there was agreement that something should be done, and quickly.

The opportunity came sooner than I imagined when my friend Joe Segal informed me that he was to host a dinner for Paul Cellucci, the U.S. ambassador to Canada. As I was chair of The Board of Trade, Joe asked me to give a speech at the dinner. The speech turned into a letter that was delivered to

Ambassador Cellucci at that dinner. The letter talked about how frustrated The Vancouver Board of Trade was with the insults and the damage they were doing to Canada-U.S. relations.

Almost immediately, the media picked up on the story, and the next morning, the letter ended up on the front page of *The Vancouver Sun,* sparking a news event that spread like wildfire, not only across the country, but over the border into the U.S. as well. The requests for media interviews flowed like a river, along with noisy threats from those who opposed our position. For the most part, I believe the membership of The Board of Trade supported the move, as did thousands of Canadians who wrote messages of encouragement.

The letter I wrote to Ambassador Cellucci gave me a very real sense of what it feels like to be in the eye of the storm and it certainly instilled in me a new appreciation for the role that Darcy Rezac plays as managing director of The Board.

The lesson I learned from the experience is this: When you find yourself in the eye of the storm, unless you have a set of values that guide you, you can easily find yourself walking the plank of public opinion.

The memories I have of my time as chair of The Board of Trade will last me a lifetime. It was a great opportunity to move outside of my comfort zone.

Here are 10 more leadership ideas:

Add a personal touch to your leadership style

Day-to-day life is hectic, especially in the business world, but that's not an excuse for not taking the time to get to know the people you work for and with. Making a personal investment of your time will pay off. When you venture beyond perfunctory "hellos" to heartfelt greetings, you send out a message of acceptance that will encourage people to open up and share both their ideas and their talent for the benefit of all.

Learn to listen

As a leader, the ability to listen to the expectations, plans and hopes of employees, customers and other stakeholders in an active, thoughtful and critical way is essential. Active listening requires you to ask questions, challenge opinions and request clarifications. Being thoughtful means not jumping to conclusions.

It also means setting aside your own biases and giving due consideration to the ideas of others. Being able to listen critically allows you to identify potential areas of conflict before they become major problems. Think of listening as a learning opportunity. After all, how will you understand what people need from you as a leader if you're not listening?

Give direction

Leadership is never given, but leadership is always recognized. The world is in need of leaders, as are churches, countries, businesses, provinces, families.

When you give direction to your colleagues, your clients, your employees or your children, you are telling them you believe in their capabilities, that they can achieve. Once you give direction, get out of the way and let people perform.

Good manners never go out of style

Be courteous to all around you, regardless of rank or position. Manners are a way of communicating respect, and everyone deserves respect. In a major survey of corporations, the most common complaint of support personnel was the failure on the part of management to acknowledge their presence other than to issue orders. It is a culture of caring, as well as common courtesies, that helps to bond a team. As a leader, you are always "on stage" modelling behaviour for those you lead. Remember to smile and make eye contact when you are speaking with someone and it only takes a moment to say thank you for a job well done.

You don't always get what you want

You work hard and, darn it, you deserve recognition, right? Unfortunately, life won't always hand you what you think you deserve. Sometimes you just have to persevere, even when awards and praise don't come your way. Perhaps you weren't nominated for entrepreneur of the year or employee of the month, as you thought you should be — don't let that stop you. Don't pursue recognition, pursue excellence.

Labels are for products, not people

The labels you stamp on another person will not only characterize your relationship to that person, in many instances, if you have power and they don't, it will also limit their potential for development. Therefore, be cautious of thinking, "Hey, she's just an assistant." Keep in mind, people move in many different circles.

For instance, although an assistant may not have status in your organization, that same assistant may be on the board of directors of a community organization and their expertise could be very useful to your organization. Likewise, an attitude of "I don't have to do that, I'm the boss" in regards to less glamorous tasks limits your opportunity to gain perspective and develop a "can do" work environment. No job is beneath a true leader.

Holding out for a hero

A hero, unlike a celebrity, is someone who triumphs over a great challenge — and through their actions, makes the world a better place. Don't underestimate the potential of anyone on your team. When the pressure is on, any one of them may be the hero who rises to the occasion. It is easy to rely on your "best people" when it's time for action, but remember, today's rookie could, and should, be tomorrow's star performer. That will only happen if you provide them opportunities to test themselves.

Oh Lord, it's hard to be humble

Many of the modern-day heroes or leaders we look up to are anything but humble, especially if you set your "leader meter" by today's sports personalities. With the multimillion-dollar salaries come egos to match.

The problem with ego is it leaves no room for growth, and rather than being a role model for young people, it makes one a target for those who would see them fall from their high horse. As the saying goes, "Humility is only a short fall away."

According to Stephen Covey in *First Things First*, "Humility is truly the mother of all virtues. It makes us a vessel, a vehicle, an agent instead of 'the source' or the principal. It unleashes all other learning, all growth and process."

In leadership, strive to be a person that you yourself could look up to. Mohandas K. Gandhi put it clearly: "It is unwise to be too sure of one's own wisdom. It is healthy to be reminded that the strongest might weaken and the wisest might err."

Never turn down an opportunity to learn from others

I read a story recently about a fellow who takes this philosophy seriously. Whenever he has a few idle moments with another person, whether it is a child, adult, customer, business associate, close friend, acquaintance or even a stranger waiting for the elevator, he makes this request of them,

"Teach me something." He says it is amazing what you can learn standing in the checkout line at the grocery: "Older ladies know all sorts of things that I don't."

Life is a laboratory of leadership

All too often we look to a university or MBA program to teach us about leadership when, in fact, life is a laboratory of leadership. If you are just willing to take the time to stop and pay attention, the people you meet every day will teach you enduring lessons.

There are many styles of leaders — the conductor of the orchestra, the coach, the community organizer and the visionary, to name only a few. We can learn from all of them. During my lifetime, I have spent many years at school, attended dozens of seminars, read hundreds of books and been introduced to thousands of terrific people. I acquired leadership skills from all of them, but it is the people I remember the most. Don't forget, in addition to being a leader, you are also a teacher, friend, role model and mentor. Play each part to its potential.

Learn to be a leader on your own runway.

CHAPTER 20

What I Learned at the World Economic Forum

In January 2003, my wife Kay and I made our first, and probably only, trip to the World Economic Forum (WEF) in Davos, Switzerland. For those of you who haven't heard of the WEF, think of it this way; what the Olympics is to sport, Davos is to commerce.

Essentially, it is where the statesmen and superstar CEOs, such as Bill Gates, Michael Dell and Carly Fiorina, meet up with religious and social leaders like UN secretary general Kofi Annan to swap visions and address issues that affect the global community.

So there I was, sitting in the British Airways First Class Lounge, flipping through the list of delegates, and I have to tell you that I was more than just a little daunted by the calibre of the people I'd be meeting. Bill Clinton was going to be there, and Colin Powell, John Ashcroft, Paul Martin, Allan Rock, the CEOs of Dow Corning, of Boeing, Dupont, Fedex,

Goldman Sachs, Cisco, Sun . . . and that was just the first page of the program.

Now why, you might ask, was a little guy from British Columbia, who owns a regional publishing company, on the guest list for the biggest annual economic forum in the world?

Well, when I became chair of The Vancouver Board of Trade in June 2002, I discovered one of the honours of the job included this trip to Davos. A second part of that honour was me paying my own way, but that's another story, and in retrospect, it was a small price to pay for the experience. The point of going to the WEF was to bring ideas back to Vancouver and to boost the city's profile among the world's who's who.

For me, being in Davos with kings, queens, knights and bishops was like playing chess live. It was a networking experience that unless you were privileged to go, you couldn't possibly fathom.

Before the forum began, managing director of The Board of Trade Darcy Rezac told me to dress every day as if I was going to a formal dinner. I soon understood why. Between breakfast at 8 a.m. and the dinner meetings at 8 p.m., running back to the hotel wasn't an option. In any case, I wouldn't have wanted to miss a moment of the forum.

On one afternoon, Darcy introduced me to Robert Mundell, the Maple Ridge native who now teaches economics at Columbia University. Mundell won the Nobel Prize in 1999 for his theories on monetary and fiscal policies. And the next day he introduced me to Stanley Prusiner, the University of California professor of neurology and biochemistry, casually mentioning that Dr. Prusiner had also won the Nobel Prize. "Oh," I asked, "what for?" "For his work on Mad Cow Disease," Darcy said. "He was one of the guys who essentially discovered it."

The WEF is that kind of event. You don't run into people who attended Harvard, you run into Larry Summers, president of Harvard. I have to admit the first few days were intimidating. I went there to represent The Vancouver Board of Trade, but I'm also Peter Legge, president and CEO of a $25-million-Cdn-a-year business. That sounds great until you run into Philip Condit, CEO of the $58-billion-US-a-year Boeing, or Carly Fiorina, the boss of Hewlett-Packard ($48 billion US per year). Of course, Darcy put it into perspective for me when he pointed out, "Everybody here is a somebody and you wouldn't be here if you weren't one too."

Beyond the networking, the theme in Davos for 2003 was *Building Trust*, a reference of course to the accounting scandals, bear markets, threats of terrorism and possibility of war that overshadow the events of our daily lives. That uncertainty was at the forefront of many sessions.

Perhaps Malaysian prime minister Mahathir Mohamad summed it up best when he said, "We are now afraid to do all sorts of things, but how do we overcome this fear?" It's a tough question, and unfortunately there are no easy answers, even, I discovered, from the world's most powerful, privileged and influential people.

It is interesting, and indeed sad, that at a time when we find ourselves more interdependent than ever because of globalization, and in greater need of trust, that it is the one element most lacking in our world.

According to leadership expert and management professor James O'Toole, "Trust is the most elusive and fragile aspect of leadership." O'Toole spoke to the WEF the year before in New York following the terrorist attacks at the World Trade Center, and his message resonates even more today.

"Trust is the glue that binds people together in groups," said O'Toole. "Whenever followers are asked what they require of leaders, trust is always at the top of the list. But leaders can't provide trust directly to followers. The hitch is that trust is an outcome of all the accumulated actions and behaviours of leaders. Hence, leaders can't *do* trust."

In his speech to the WEF, O'Toole went on to say that when leaders are candid, open, consistent and predictable in their dealings, the result will almost always be a condition of trust. But that such consistency is difficult for many leaders to maintain because it requires the relatively rare trait of integrity.

"People with integrity mean what they say and practice what they preach," said O'Toole. "The prevailing ideology of leadership — contingency theory — unwittingly leads to the creation of mistrust because it encourages leaders to shift course arbitrarily and to do whatever they think is expedient to achieve their goals, including going back on their word. To renege on one's word may seem necessary to some leaders, but in the eyes of followers it is always viewed as a betrayal of trust."

I think this message is an important one for all of us, whether we are leading a country, a corporation, a committee or a family. O'Toole hit a bull's-eye with his closing remark, "The fact is that trust must be earned. And it is hard to earn, easy to lose and, once lost, nearly impossible to regain."

On the last afternoon of the forum, I spoke briefly with Bill Gates. He had just announced that he would be donating $200 million US, through his personal foundation, to global health issues. I was happily surprised when I met him; in contrast to his reputation of being brash and arrogant, he seemed very soft-spoken and almost shy. He is an inspiring figure to be sure.

Later that night as I was packing my bags in preparation for the long flight home, I thought about what I had learned from this experience that I could share with the membership of The Board of Trade. I realized if there was one thing I could take home with me from the WEF it was the sense of the possibilities, the wide-open opportunities that emerge when you put all of those people from around the globe in one room — when you pair a committed philanthropist like Gates with a scientist like Stanley Prusiner; or an entrepreneur like myself or fellow British Columbians Brandt Louie and Jay Taylor with the heads of investment banks and presidents of countries.

It was an intense five days and I am grateful to have had that brief peek behind the scenes. Whether we are privileged enough to attend or not, I believe the WEF provides a unique opportunity for dialogue, and that is something we need more of in this world if we are to have any hope of resolving our greatest conflicts.

I came home to Vancouver with a deeper appreciation for the relationship I have with my mentor Joe Segal. When it comes to business and philanthropy, Joe plays on the same field as the powerful men and women I met at the WEF, yet I know that I can call him up anytime to have lunch and ask for his wisdom. For that, I consider myself truly fortunate. It's also a good reminder that we don't have to travel around the world looking for leaders or heroes. They walk among us, and if we are willing to put in the necessary effort to learn from their experience, they are more than willing to share their knowledge.

CHAPTER 21

Blue Skies Ahead

So why do I close a motivational book with a story about the World Economic Forum in Davos — a small ski village two and a half hours by train from Zurich? I believe life in general, and our own runway of life in particular, is full of exciting opportunities if we would just look and see the doors and windows that open for us almost every day.

As I've quoted Benjamin Franklin in a previous chapter, we have a long time to sleep when we are dead. So for us to lead a meaningful life, or better yet, a life of significance; and to experience life and all it has to offer, we need to engage in activities that enrich us, so that we are able to better serve the world we live in and grow as citizens of a fragile planet. We need to experience as much as we can and have the courage to walk through those doors and windows that open for us.

One of the very best business decisions I have ever made was accepting the invitation of Carole Taylor, now chair of the Canadian Broadcasting Corporation, and The

Vancouver Board of Trade's managing director, Darcy Rezac, to take on the chairman's position at The Board of Trade . . . phew! What a challenge, and yes, at the outset it was very intimidating.

Some of Vancouver's finest business men and women have served the 4,500-plus member-based business association over the years with great distinction. Names like Bob Kadlec, P.Eng, vice-chairman of the Eaton Power Corporation; Bob Stewart, president of Scott Paper; Rick Turner, president and CEO of International Aviation Terminals Inc., now involved with the 2010 Olympic Games to be held in Vancouver and Whistler; Wendy MacDonald, chair of BC Bearing Engineers Ltd.; Brandt Louie, president of London Drugs and the 100-year-old grocery company H.Y. Louie Co. Ltd.; and Jill Bodkin, chair of Golden Heron Enterprises and director of The Laurentian Bank of Canada.

What on earth could I bring to this most distinguished organization? What leadership skills could I share in my year in office? Could I afford the time away from my own business? What would happen to my professional speaking career? I would have to withdraw from engagements further away from Vancouver than Kelowna, Victoria or Calgary. What else would I have to sacrifice? Would my wife and children support this extremely busy year? Could I handle the pressure of countless meetings, policy forums, cocktail parties, luncheons and dozens and dozens of speeches (that was about the only challenge I felt comfortable with)?

The list of reasons why I shouldn't or couldn't do the job seemed endless. I was defeating myself before I had even begun. Then it hit me. Carole and Darcy thought I could do the job. Surely they weren't just acting on a hunch. Others must have been in on this decision. They must have researched my credentials and my standing in the community.

So, with the full blessing of my wife and children, I humbly accepted the position as chairman of The Vancouver Board of Trade with a resolution to be the very best chair I could possibly be — to chair every executive meeting, every full Board meeting, attend a minimum of 150 Board-related events and go with my wife to Davos. I had to risk and seize the opportunity that lay before me and walk through the door that had just opened.

I reflected once again on the words of my Speakers Roundtable colleague Charlie "Tremendous" Jones: "We will be the same person today in five years except for the people we meet, the places we go and the books we read." I was about to meet *a lot* of people.

As I look back on my life, almost every advance in my career has been a series of door openings that something inside me has prompted me to walk through. Dr. Robert Schuller, who shares Toastmasters' most coveted speaking award with me, The Golden Gavel Award, said, "It is better to try at something and fail than to try at nothing and succeed."

Very often, the special opportunities come around just once in our life and we don't want to die with the music still in us. Therefore, we must risk.

Here are some examples from my own life of the once-in-a-lifetime opportunities that I have seized and am truly thankful for.

• I was invited to speak in the House of Commons in Ottawa during the National Prayer Breakfast.

• In 1988, I flew on the Concorde from London's Heathrow to New York's Kennedy airport. The Concorde doesn't exist now.

• My wife and I were thrilled to interview HRH Queen Elizabeth's private secretary in Buckingham Palace.

• On behalf of the Red Cross, I invited the exiled King of Rwanda to Vancouver for a fundraising campaign to aid the King's country and raised almost a million dollars in the process. As a result, in April 1997, the Red Cross Society of Canada presented me with The Order of the Red Cross.

• My daughter Rebecca and I were privileged to have lunch at Kensington Palace with the Prince and Princess of Kent.

• At the Variety International Humanitarian Award in Chicago, I met Sammy Davis Jr.

• On a press trip to London arranged by the British Travel Association, I visited the home of Sir Winston Churchill (Chartwell in Kent) where our group of six had a private tour of the estate.

• On another press trip, my wife and I travelled from New York to Southampton on the magnificent ocean liner, *QE II.*

Now just in case you are saying right about now, "Well,

sure, Peter, you've had all these grand experiences because of your business and your connections." And that is true, but these things were not handed to me. The truth is, I came from a working-class family where the only real advantages I had were opportunity and encouragement. My business and connections are the result of many years of commitment and dedication. Not bad for a kid from England, who was the grandson of a railway porter and a scullery maid.

The point I would like to make from this is that we all need to walk through the doors that open for us, because there really are amazing opportunities to be found on the other side. Think about your own list of once-in-a-lifetime opportunities. Write them down and put the list in a place where you can review and add to them often.

We all have our own unique dreams to follow. One of my wife's dreams was to graduate from university. She had spent the first 15 years of our marriage as an at-home mom attending our three daughters. A conscious decision that paid off; we have three spectacular daughters. So it was that the fear of failure and her then-current age almost prevented her from getting her undergraduate degree and then moving on to her Masters in Counselling from Trinity Western University.

When she first considered going back to university, Kay was quite doubtful. I remember she came to me and said, "It's going to take me six years and I will be almost 50 when I graduate." I told her, "In six years you will be 50 anyway, so why not go for it?" Today she is a therapist specializing in marriage counselling at a clinic just outside of Vancouver.

Of course, it is not just the fear of failure that holds us back, it is also the fear of success. Fear of success is often linked to a feeling of being out of our depth or a misguided belief that we don't deserve to be successful. Either way, both types of fear stop us in our tracks and we end up saying, "If only."

I can't even begin to tell you what sort of life I might have lived if my father, at the age of 16, had not run away to sea on a cargo ship — run by the Reardon Smith line out of Cardiff, Wales — called *MS Vancouver City.* He climbed aboard the ship at the Barry docks in South Wales just seven miles from Cardiff and it was the beginning of his first adventure.

During those years, my father visited the port of Vancouver several times as a crew member. Later, those visits would play a role in my parents' decision to emigrate to Vancouver, Canada. Amazingly, six months after he left the *MS Vancouver City,* she was sunk in the English Channel by Nazi U-Boats during the Second World War. And shortly after that, my father came to Canada.

I often wonder if my father's risk-taking has rubbed off on me. He always told me his move to Canada was the making of his life and it provided an opportunity for his only son.

Sow an act and you reap a habit. Sow a habit and reap a character. Sow a character and you reap a destiny for yourself, your family and your world. The bible is clear in Luke 11, verses 9 and 10, "Ask and it will be given to you. Seek and you will find. Knock and the door will be opened for you."

So I urge you, if you have read this far, take courage, rev up your engines and head down that runway — your runway. There are plenty of blue skies ahead. And remember, if our runway of life goes on until we are 85 years of age, we have just 4,420 weeks to experience all of life's challenges and unique opportunities.

Life is for the taking. Hippocrates' wise words, which I quoted in Chapter 2, are worth repeating: "The life so short, the craft so hard to learn." And William Shakespeare noted, "What is past is prologue."

So make the most of the tomorrows, every tomorrow, by making the most of today. Good luck. Carpe Diem!

ABOUT THE AUTHOR

Dr. Peter Legge, LL.D (HON) • CSP • CPAE • H.O.F.

Peter Legge is president and CEO of Canada Wide Magazines & Communications Ltd., the largest independently owned publishing company in Western Canada, controlling a network of 31 magazines across the country with over $25 million in sales annually.

In addition, Peter travels the world as a motivational speaker, accepting more than 100 assignments each year from clients who know that when he speaks, his words will be a catalyst for positive change. He has received the prestigious Golden Gavel Award from Toastmasters International and was voted "Top Speaker in North America," in company with Dr. Robert Schuller and Stephen Covey. Peter has also been inducted into the Speakers Hall of Fame by both the National Speakers Association and the Canadian Association of Professional Speakers.

Peter is tireless in his commitments to many worthwhile organizations. As co-host of the annual Variety Telethon for more than 26 years, he has assisted in raising more than $100 million for the charity. He is also an International Ambassador of Variety International.

His efforts have not gone unnoticed. Among his many honours, Peter has received the Golden Heart Award from the Variety Club and has been invested into the Venerable Order of St. John of Jerusalem. He has been awarded the Order of the Red Cross and named Citizen of the Year for his commitment to the community. He was recently inducted into the Canadian Sales Hall of Fame. Simon Fraser University has honoured him with an Honorary Doctor of Laws Degree, and he was chair of the Vancouver Board of Trade in 2003.

Peter is also the author of six previous books that have inspired thousands of readers the world over with their powerful motivating messages. In all that he has achieved, Peter attributes his success to three factors: persistence, patience and a positive attitude.

To contact Peter Legge, and have him speak at your next conference, write to:
Peter Legge Management Company
4180 Lougheed Highway, 4th Floor
Burnaby, B.C. V5C 6A7
Canada
Telephone: 604-299-7311
E-mail plegge@canadawide.com

ORDER FORM

No	Description	Qty	Price	Total
B100	The Runway of Life *Hard Cover*		29.95 CDN 25.95 U.S.	
B101	If Only I'd Said That: Vol. II *Hard Cover*		29.95 CDN 25.95 U.S.	
B102	Who Dares Wins *Hard Cover*		29.95 CDN 25.95 U.S.	
B103	If Only I'd Said That: Vol. I *Hard Cover*		29.95 CDN 25.95 U.S.	
B104	97 Tips on Business* *Booklet*		4.97 CDN 3.97 U.S.	
B105	97 Tips on Customer Service* *Booklet*		4.97 CDN 3.97 U.S.	
B106	97 Tips to Jump-start Your Career* *Booklet*		4.97 CDN 3.97 U.S.	
	Videotapes			
V101	How To Soar With The Eagles* (90 mins.)		30.00 CDN 25.00 U.S.	
V102	"Live" in Orlando* (60 mins.)		30.00 CDN 25.00 U.S.	
	Subtotal			
	Shipping and handling		5.00 CDN 3.00 U.S.	
	Subtotal			
	Canadian Residents add 7% GST			
	BC Residents Add 7.5% PST *(videotapes & booklets only)			
	TOTAL			

For faster service FAX your credit card order to **(604) 299-9188**
or call **(604) 299-7311**

PAYMENT

☐ Cheque payable to Peter Legge Management Co. Ltd.

☐ Please charge $________________ to my MasterCard/Visa (CIRCLE ONE)

CC# ____________________________________Expiry Date_____________________

Signature ________________________________

Please send my order to: (PLEASE PRINT)

Name____Tel__________________

Address____

City___________________________Prov/State __________Postal/Zip___________

Peter Legge Management Co. Ltd., 4th Floor, 4180 Lougheed Hwy., Burnaby, B.C. V5C 6A7 Canada